MW01286484

NEBRASKA

THE PROGRAM

A Curated History of the Huskers

SEAN CALLAHAN

TRIUMPH
BOOKS

Library of Congress Cataloging-in-Publication Data

Names: Callahan, Sean, 1965—author.
Title: The program Nebraska : a curated history of the Huskers / Sean Callahan.
Other titles: Curated history of the Huskers
Description: Chicago, Illinois : Triumph Books LLC, [2025] | Series: The franchise | Identifiers: LCCN 2024044691 | ISBN 9781637276129 (cloth)
Subjects: LCSH: University of Nebraska—Lincoln—Football—History. | Nebraska Cornhuskers (Football team)—History.
Classification: LCC GV958.U53 C354 2025 | DDC 796.332/6309782293—dc23/eng/20250402
LC record available at https://lccn.loc.gov/2024044691

This book is available in quantity at special discounts for your group or organization. For further information, contact:
  Triumph Books LLC
  814 North Franklin Street
  Chicago, Illinois 60610
  (312) 337-0747
  www.triumphbooks.com

Printed in U.S.A.
ISBN: 978-1-63727-612-9
Design by Preston Pisellini
Page production by Nord Compo

To my daughters, Kit and Carly Callahan,
don't let anyone ever tell you it can't be done.
Always believe and bet on yourself.
Hard work and perseverance will win out.

To my wife, Lisa Callahan, thank you for understanding
and supporting me and everything that comes with this job.

CONTENTS

Part 3 The Traditions

Part 4 The Players

Part 5 The Rivalries

Foreword

In 1991 my wife, Nancy, was watching a segment of *60 Minutes* on television. She was impressed by a story involving an elderly businessman named Eugene Lang who had been invited back to address the eighth grade graduation ceremony at the middle school he had attended years before.

Mr. Lang was surprised at the changes, which had occurred since he had gone to school there. He asked the principal of the school how many young people were likely to go on to college. He was shocked when the principal said that he thought that maybe one student would eventually attend college. When Lang had gone to school there, nearly every student planned to attend college. When he addressed the students, he departed from his prepared remarks and told the students that if they stayed out of trouble and graduated from high school, he would pay their way to college.

Nancy was impressed and asked if we could do something similar. I was in my 18th year as head coach at the University of Nebraska and was making a decent salary but far short of what coaches are paid today. So I knew that putting a school of children through college was out of reach. I told her I would see what I could do. So the next day I got up in front of the Nebraska football team and asked how many of them would be willing to volunteer to serve as a mentor for some seventh- and eighth-grade boys in Lincoln, Nebraska, schools. Twenty-two hands went up. We matched the players with 22 young men whom school officials identified as young men who could use a mentor. Nancy and Barb Hopkins, a school administrator, made sure that the players met with their mentees once a week, and once a month, the whole group got together, played some basketball, ate pizza, and listened to speakers who discussed various life skills.

Things went smoothly, but after a couple of years, I realized that many of these mentees were approaching 16 years of age, an age when young people could drop out of school at that time. I was concerned so I got in front of the group and told the mentees that if they stayed out of trouble and graduated from high school we would pay their way to college (similar to Lang but on a much smaller scale).

The only problem with this was that I did not know where the money was going to come from. It turned out that a large amount of money had been raised at a banquet recognizing 200 football wins—100 under Bob Devaney, the coach preceding me, and 100 wins under me. The University Foundation agreed that this money could be put to use for TeamMates scholarships for those who went to college in the university system.

As time went on, we were gratified when 21 of the 22 mentees graduated from high school on time and 18 went on to college. The one mentee who did not graduate high school on time graduated a year later, as he had been racing on a moto-cross circuit. We were very surprised at these numbers as we thought that if 15 or so of the young men graduated from high school and four or five went on to college that would have represented significant improvement.

Mentees were not the only beneficiaries of mentoring. The football players serving as mentors enjoyed serving someone who could not on the surface do anything for them in return. They learned that giving the gift of time is the most precious gift anyone can give. We can make more money, but none of us can make more time. Serving and giving adds a measure of meaning and purpose to life. Some of those players are still in touch with their mentees now—more than 30 years later.

The reason I asked our football players to mentor was not just about Nancy being impressed by Lang's story. I started coaching in 1962 as a graduate assistant coach at the University of Nebraska. As the years passed, I saw some alarming trends impacting young people. In the early 1960s, we seldom recruited a young man who was not living with both biological parents. As time went on, we had many of our players coming from single-parent families, and even a few who had no parents in their lives. We began to deal with not only football, but also more personal issues resulting from a lack of parenting.

Today more than half of our young people are growing up without both biological parents. I have come to believe that the No. 1 problem facing the United States today is not something with the economy, foreign affairs, immigration, etc. It is the breakdown of the family. More and more young people need a caring adult in their lives, someone who cares about them unconditionally and will be a consistent source of support.

In the late 1970s and early 1980s, we saw the advent of the drug culture. Woodstock, Timothy Leary, LSD, marijuana, cocaine came on the scene. Eventually, we began to drug test our players, something we would not have considered just a few years earlier. Today very few young people go through middle school without the opportunity to partake of some illegal substance. The few players, who eventually were dismissed from the team because of substance abuse, nearly always began using in middle school and could not shake the habit.

We also saw a shift in the entertainment industry. Much of the content of movies, television, music lyrics, and later social media would not have appeared in the public domain 20 or 30 years ago. It is hard for young people to sort their way through this confusing and sometimes destructive information.

Because of Nancy's inspiration from the Lang story and my own observations with our football players, we decided to expand TeamMates. We began in Lincoln and used adults over age 18 as mentors. We then went across Nebraska and then expanded into Iowa, Kansas, South Dakota, and Wyoming. We are currently serving approximately 10,000 young people annually.

The TeamMates model is fairly simple. Our mentoring is one to one and is school based. All mentoring, which spans third through 12th grades, is done in a school setting. We have building coordinators in each school who help match mentors and mentees according to similar interests, sign mentors in and out, and make sure that there is an appropriate place in the school to meet. Much of our mentoring occurs during the lunch period, which usually lasts about 40 minutes. Meetings are flexible: if the mentor can't come on a designated day, the building coordinator finds an appropriate substitute day.

Mentors are trained on required procedures. No phone calls, emails, or text messages are allowed. If a mentee appears to be a danger to himself or herself or has a serious problem, the mentee is to be referred to an appropriate health care professional. Mentors undergo background checks and are trained in what are appropriate activities such as playing UNO, going to the gym to shoot baskets, etc. TeamMates has mentored more than 45,000 young people since inception without an incident of harm to a mentee.

We have consistently measured mentoring results over the years by gathering data. The academic results have been consistently good. We find that 80 to 85 percent of our mentees show improved attendance and behavior. Grades improve, and our graduation rate from high school has consistently been at 95 percent or better. Last year our graduation rate was 98 percent, and we graduated 830 mentees. Since the majority of our mentees are from single-parent families and live below the poverty line, we believe that we are graduating at least 100 or more young people who would not have graduated if they had not had a mentor. The average high school dropout costs society $300,000 in their lifetime in social costs such as incarceration, unemployment benefits, substance abuse treatment, etc. If my assumptions are correct—and I believe that they are very conservative—this would represent a savings of $30 million annually.

I am so proud of what we've done at TeamMates, and it's something that wouldn't have been possible without the University of Nebraska's charity. This is a great school and a special program. In this book Sean Callahan weaves together the wonderful people, inspiring leaders, special athletes, and unique traditions that make the Huskers the program we enjoy rooting for.

—Tom Osborne

PART 1

THE COACHES

1

Tom Osborne

In January of 1962, Tom Osborne's life was at a crossroads. The Hastings, Nebraska, native had just finished his three-year career as a wide receiver in the NFL. Before that he was a standout quarterback at Hastings College. He was looking for a fresh start after an injury ended his pro football career. "I've been in [the] NFL for three years with the 49ers and then Redskins," Osborne said. "I had a pulled hamstring, and they kept shooting it with Novocain, which is not a good practice. Eventually, I had enough scar tissue in there that I didn't think I could play anymore."

So, what was next for Osborne? School. He decided to enroll in graduate classes for the second semester at the University of Nebraska. Newly-named head coach Bob Devaney was also in his first full month at Nebraska. Osborne had never met Devaney, nor did he have any connections to his coaching staff, but he wanted to see if there were any coaching opportunities.

It's not uncommon for new head coaches to have people knock on their doors looking for opportunities. Osborne was probably one of several that approached Devaney at that time.

Devaney's staff had no coaching opportunities at the full-time or graduate assistant level. Then Devaney realized he might have something. He needed somebody to manage a group of rowdy student-athletes in the Selleck Quadrangle dorm building. This was far from a glamourous job for the former Nebraska state high school (1955) and college athlete of the year (1959), but Osborne took it. This was his foot in the door.

Little did anyone know at the time that Devaney's decision to offer Osborne an opportunity to babysit a rowdy dorm floor would be the start of a decision that would change this state and the history of college football forever. It only took Devaney a few months to realize he had a potential rising star in the coaching industry on his hands. "I came back from Redskins. We played the last game in December. I came in back and enrolled for the second semester, which would've been the start of 1962," Osborne said. "I arrived at just about the same time that Bob did because he'd been hired from Wyoming. I went in to see him. I just thought I would miss athletics. I was going to go into college administration work and work on a PhD. I thought, *Well, maybe I could be a graduate assistant football coach and somehow satisfy the athletic side of things and still do my graduate work.* When I first went in and see him, he said, 'I had all the coaches' he needed. Then he said, 'I understand there's a lot of problems over in Selleck Quadrangle.' Marquette had dropped football. We brought in four or five guys from Marquette, and they are Chicago-area guys. They had thrown the dorm counselor out on their floor and they're running the show.

"Bob said, 'If you'd move in over there and ride hard on things,' he said, 'I'll give you meals on the training table.'

"I moved in there and I run it with a guy named Jerry Spears. Jerry was from Ohio and was a basketball player. The rest of them were football players. I break up a few fights and I remember they were going to throw Larry Kramer out of school because he had thrown a snowball inside Selleck Quadrangle. He'd taken a newspaper and he hadn't paid for it. They wanted to throw him out of school. I went to the disciplinary council with Larry and tried to lay out a case that would be a little bit extreme. Larry stayed in school, and I think Bob appreciated that. Anyway, when spring ball came around, he said, 'Well, I think we could probably use you out there.' It was mostly [because of] that experience with those players that he felt he'd give me a shot."

Devaney has said before that one of his real strengths as a head coach was that he knew how to hire great people around him. He had a staff of several guys who would become eventual head coaches at places like Miami, North Carolina State, Washington State, and Iowa State. There was something about Osborne that Devaney knew was different. "Tom worked hard at it," Mike Devaney, the son of Bob Devaney, said. "He was up there a lot of times with my dad looking at films and stuff like that. He was always a student of the game as well. I think that my dad always appreciated his hard work and especially the fact that he was also going to school, which reminded him of his endeavors as he was trying to get an education. I think that he always respected Tom's creativity as an offensive mind. I think he thought Tom had one of the best offensive minds that he had ever met in his whole coaching career."

After three seasons as a graduate assistant coach, Bob Devaney quickly realized he did not want to lose the young Osborne to another school. Devaney elevated Osborne to a full-time coach in 1964; by 1969 he was calling the plays for Nebraska's offense. From 1969 to 1997, Osborne would go on to call every single offensive play at Nebraska, including on five national championship teams and seven that played in bowl games for the national title.

* * *

Every head coach is going to experience his ups and downs. After Bob Devaney began his time at Nebraska with appearances in the Gotham, Orange, Cotton, Orange, and Sugar Bowls over his first five years, his program experienced back-to-back 6–4 seasons. Nebraska's passionate fanbase was quickly getting spoiled by the early success Devaney brought the program, and back-to-back 6–4 seasons in 1967 and 1968 weren't going to cut it.

Devaney was chasing his rival, Bear Bryant. The Alabama Crimson Tide had beaten the Cornhuskers in back-to-back seasons in the Orange and Cotton Bowls, including a 34–7 thumping to end the 1966 season.

What was Devaney's response? He tried to build his team like Bryant did at Alabama.

"They had gotten to recruiting high school fullbacks and linebackers and made offensive linemen out of them. Their linemen were 190, 200, 205 pounds, and they were quick kids and they scramble blocked," Tom Osborne said. "We got side-tracked and went down that path, and it didn't work for us. Our offensive line really just wasn't able to move people. I told Bob, 'Maybe it'd be a good idea if we went out to California and tried to recruit some junior college players because we needed some immediate help.' And, of course, the conventional wisdom was the California kids would never come to Nebraska. I did get some players. Bob Newton came in, Dick Rupert, Bob Terry was a linebacker, and then Carl Johnson and Keith Wortman. Those kids all started for us on the offensive line, and three of them went to the NFL. I think that got Bob thinking a little bit. We had been running an unbalanced line, full-house backfield, which he'd brought with him from Michigan State to Wyoming, and it seemed like people caught up with that. He thought we'd make a change and he asked me to do it. I don't know what he saw in me, but at least he gave me a chance."

Osborne then convinced Devaney to move Nebraska to the I-formation on offense. They saw immediate results. The next thing he did was introduce Devaney to a little-known NU track athlete named Boyd Epley, who took up the sport of weightlifting. Epley showed Osborne what could be done if athletes were properly trained in the weight room and the advancements they make even in the recovery process.

Osborne took Epley to Devaney, and the brash Devaney gave him an opportunity. He was paid minimum wage and named the first strength coach in the history of college athletics. "[Boyd] said, 'I could really help the football team,'" Osborne said. "Boyd had gotten into weightlifting and he'd gotten bigger. He'd fallen out of favor with the track coach because he was breaking some of the pole-vaulting poles. He was a pole vaulter. I took him in to see Bob, and Boyd made the same pitch.

"He said, 'I think I can really help the football team.' Bob was from the old school where weightlifting would make you muscle-bound. Most football coaches and basketball coaches wouldn't advocate weight training because they felt it would tighten you up, stiffen you up, and make you slower. I remember Bob specifically told Boyd, 'Well, okay, we'll try it, but if it doesn't work, you're fired.' That was his opening statement.

"Boyd took over the strength training program, and some of it came from those two years where we were 6–4, and we developed an offseason program. I remember we had a circuit deal and I think Alabama had done some of that, too, since we had stations where it'd be bags, agility work, and agility ropes. I ran a cardiovascular station, and the players would be with me for six minutes, and we just ran laps around the indoor practice facility. I'd run with them, and then we had a competitive drill up in one of the handball courts. We put pads down on the floor, and they had an axe handle, and two guys grabbed the axe handle and tried to take it away from each other. It got pretty rough up there."

The results came quickly. In 1968 Oklahoma beat Nebraska 47–0 in Norman on national television. By 1969 Osborne ran Devaney's new I-formation offense and helped oversee Epley's strength program. Things looked much different when the Huskers faced the Sooners at Memorial Stadium in Lincoln in 1969. NU won 44–14, and the Devaney era turned another corner. They were poised to break out as a national power in 1970. "We ended up 9–2, had a pretty good year, and then in 1970 and 1971 won championships," Osborne said. "In about 1970 he told me he was going to just become AD. Then we had pretty good years, and he said he'd like to see if we could win three in a row. He stayed on in 1972. I was named assistant head coach and then took over in 1973. That's how it all transpired. Of course, he was the AD for quite some time, and I was the head football coach."

After Devaney captured the 1970 national championship, he already began to think about his next move. Osborne had shown him a lot. He revamped the offense, changed NU's recruiting approach, and helped implement college athletics' first ever offseason strength and conditioning program.

Assistant coach Jim Walden was close to Devaney. He played for him at Wyoming and was on the staff at Nebraska. By the spring of 1971, he realized Osborne was going to succeed Devaney. "I'm riding out to Grand Island, Nebraska, with Coach Devaney," Walden said. "I'm driving; he's got to make a speech."

At the get-together, someone had asked Walden if Devaney was going to quit. "Well, on the way home, I threw that out," Walden said. "He said to me, 'Jim, I'm not sure I'm thinking about quitting.' He said, 'I'm not sure I'm going to quit, but I'm thinking about it.'

"I said, 'Well, hey, you have that right. You've got a great job. You're doing two jobs.'

"He said, 'Well, I haven't been a head coach that long. I've had enough success in the years that I've done it and since I am the AD I have a backup. I'm going roll along with it.'

"I said, 'Well, is there anybody, any particular person? Are you going to try to hire from within, Coach? Or are you going to maybe tell the guys that you want to go out from outside?'

"He said, 'No, I'm leaning toward one of our guys inside.'

"I said, 'Well, I pretty well know who that is.' I didn't say his name, but he didn't reflect back that it wasn't. I think Carl Selmer thought it might be him, but I knew it wasn't. Carl did not have the temperament at all. He had a really great temperament for an offensive line coach, but he didn't have the temperament, in my opinion, to be a head coach. He proved that at Miami. I don't think Mike Corgan would have taken it. Jim Ross wasn't going to take it. Well, then that only left John Melton, and he wasn't going to take it. There was just the three young bucks. That was me, Warren Powers, and Monte Kiffin. I just felt like we didn't have the feeling that Devaney would leave the program to either one of us compared to Tom. That's just me, and so I wasn't surprised when he announced the next year that he was going to coach the '72 season, but he had already announced that Tom was going to be the new head coach."

Mike Devaney said that Osborne's interview for a head coaching job at Texas Tech got his father's attention. Serving as both the AD and head coach starting in 1967, Devaney knew Osborne was the right guy to succeed him. "My dad promised him in '72 after they won that championship that nobody had ever won three championships in a row," Devaney said. "He said, 'If you'll let me coach one more year,' he says, 'I'll make sure that you get the job.'"

The remarkable thing Osborne successfully did was follow a legend. You can count on one hand the number of coaches that have replaced a legend and then experienced that same type of winning during their tenure.

Osborne did that, but it wasn't all wine and roses. He experienced his fair share of struggles. Having Devaney as the athletic director until 1992 and then serving as the AD emeritus from 1992 to 1996 helped Osborne survive a few rocky patches. Most notably, Osborne started his career 1–8 vs. rival Oklahoma from 1973 to 1980. He also had a span from 1987 to 1993, losing seven consecutive bowl games to end the season. "The biggest challenge was following Bob Devaney," Osborne said. "I knew a little bit about the history book. The guy following Bear Bryant didn't last very long—same way the guy who followed John McKay and Joe Paterno. I applied to a couple of places. I thought I was going to get the job at Texas Tech but came in second there, and Bob asked me to stay on, and I knew I had his backing and that was good.

"The fans weren't real sure because we lost to Oklahoma the first five times that I had coached teams against them, and it had become a one-game season. We'd win nine or 10 games, but if we didn't beat Oklahoma, it would be a bad year. It was not easygoing, but eventually, we did beat Oklahoma in '78, and then things got better after that. I survived the curse of following a very popular, very successful coach, but a lot of times, it's pretty touch and go. In my case I think if Bob hadn't been the AD that I might have gotten fired. I don't know. We had some 9–3 seasons, and I think most people say that those are pretty good years. People that have won national championships and had had a couple of undefeated seasons—then that becomes a standard."

In today's college football world, a lot of coaches may not have survived, but Osborne had the backing and support of Devaney, which was key. In some ways, Osborne later provided similar support for Bo Pelini when he was the athletic director. Once Osborne was forced to retire as AD in 2012, that opened the door for the next AD to fire Pelini after a nine-win season in 2014.

In 25 years as head coach, Osborne finished with a 255–49–3 record. He won 39 consecutive regular-season conference games from 1992 to 1997 and captured national championships in 1994, 1995, and 1997. When former Huskers wide receiver and assistant coach Guy Ingles looks back on what played out with Osborne, it truly is remarkable. "What Tom did at Nebraska, it's harder than everybody else's place," Ingles said. "There are no players here. They had to take me because they had 45 scholarships. Now, thank God, they took me. I guess I was dumb enough to go there and think I could play, that I was unusual. I was just fast enough and I could catch the ball when I was five years old, I swear. I just got lucky. I looked at my freshman football picture not too long ago, and 17 guys from Nebraska got scholarships."

Nebraska has the second lowest population out of any state that features a major conference program and it has the fewest amount of four- and five-star recruits within 500 miles of nearly any school in the country. Osborne built his program on the backs of hard-working Nebraska kids and found the right formula of out-of-state talent to blend in to compete nationally. Just think about his first national championship: a group of mostly Nebraska natives figured out a way to wear down a Miami defense that featured future NFL Hall of Famers Ray Lewis and Warren Sapp. Osborne built Nebraska and he built it the Nebraska way. There has never been a better innovator in college football history.

2

Bob Devaney

YOU MIGHT CALL 1941 TO 1961 THE DARK AGES OF NEBRASKA football. After appearing in the 1941 Rose Bowl under head coach Biff Jones, the program only experienced two winning records over the next 21 seasons. The best mark over those 21 years was a 6–5 season that got them into the 1955 Orange Bowl—only because of a Big 8 Conference "no-repeat" rule. That rule prevented 10–0 Oklahoma from playing in the Orange Bowl despite beating the Huskers 55–7 on November 20, 1954. No. 14 Duke would beat NU in the Orange Bowl 34–7.

Nebraska football was at rock bottom. Bill Jennings had five straight losing seasons before being fired in 1961. University of Nebraska chancellor Clifford Hardin was looking for a change. He came to NU after stops at Michigan State (1944–1948) and the University of Chicago. During his time in East Lansing, Michigan, he was used to seeing winning football from the Spartans. When the university parted ways with Jennings, the first person Hardin contacted for his opening at Nebraska was Michigan State head coach Duffy Daugherty, who had recently taken the Spartans to the Rose Bowl in 1955.

Daugherty declined to enter discussions with Hardin, but the next thing he did would change the history of this state forever. Daugherty recommended to Hardin a former colleague of his—Bob Devaney. A Michigan native, Devaney had just finished his fifth season at Wyoming. The Cowboys had won the Skyline Conference four years in a row under Devaney and finished ranked No. 17 in the 1961 coaches poll. Devaney racked up a 35–10–5 record in Laramie, Wyoming. "Duffy basically talked to him and said, 'Bob, if you win there, you can make No. 1 in the polls, earn a lot of money, and you will also have all the support you need to make it become a major player in the athletic community,'" Mike Devaney, Bob Devaney's son, said.

This got Bob Devaney's attention. He was the ultimate competitor. He decided to make a trip to Lincoln, Nebraska. However, since he was the sitting head coach at Wyoming, it was kept under wraps. Devaney was greeted at the airport by a group of people, including Nebraska football and eventual College Football Hall of Famer Clarence Swanson, a NU Board of Regents member. "He was the one that met Bob at the plane and was instrumental in getting Bob here," former Huskers linebacker Tom Ruud, who married Swanson's granddaughter Jaime, said. "The stories that are passed on from Jaime's aunt, who tells the story, said Clarence and a couple of other people involved in the search, were very instrumental in wanting him and convincing Bob Devaney that this would be a good place for him and a good place to have some fun."

Having fun was something Devaney had no problem finding wherever he went. He was more interested in learning about the state of Nebraska and, most importantly, the football team.

To his surprise Jennings' 3–6–1 team from 1961 had much more talent than anyone probably realized. Devaney raced back to Wyoming, excited about what he saw in Lincoln. He later accepted the job. His defensive line coach, Lloyd Eaton, stayed at Wyoming and took over for Devaney. Assistants John Melton, Mike Corgan, Jim Ross, and Carl Selmer would follow Devaney to Lincoln. "My dad, that's the reason why he went there is because it felt like maybe it would get him to another level," Mike Devaney said. "He went there incognito and looked at the films. He came back and he told me personally, 'I don't know why they're not winning football games. They got as good of athletes as we had at Michigan State…if not better.' As it turned out, 13 of those kids that were on that first team all got drafted in the top 10 rounds of the pro draft."

So what was the issue? Why could Jennings bring in such elite talent but not get it to work? "One thing he found out was that Jennings was just beating the shit out of them on the football field in practice and that they left it all there and didn't have anything left for the games," Mike Devaney recalled. "They were four-hour brutal practices, and kids were tired. They were beat up. Basically, my dad said they just left their game on the practice field. I know my dad. When he first came there, the first few practices, they had set that up after talking to everybody. They set it up and they always had a little different philosophy. They used to split the groups up into four or five different stations and they would get everybody involved in running repetitive formations and plays and stuff like that. They got a lot of people involved, and there weren't people standing around. As a result, they were able to condense the practice sessions to very short periods of time, a couple of hours or something. I remember the first few practices they had—the players couldn't believe that that was how long they were."

Former Huskers wide receiver Guy Ingles played for Devaney from 1967 to 1970 and he heard stories about the Jennings era. "They were scrimmaging on Friday. They were practicing three- and four-hour practices. They had plenty of athletes. They didn't know what to do with them," Ingles said. "Here comes Bob, and I remember talking to [Tom] Osborne, and he said, 'Bob made a commitment. I don't care, guys. These guys have been practicing three or four hours a day. We're going to be on the field no longer than two hours. I mean it. If somebody's out there after two hours, he better be a kicker or better be a quarterback or a receiver. That's about it. Everybody else is out of there.' [Quarterback] Dennis Claridge said, 'Football had been drudgery. Now, it was fun.'"

Devaney was ahead of his time in an era where most coaches had a boot camp mentality with how they ran football practices. He believed in practicing smart, which was not the norm when you go back to that era, which featured practice approaches like how Bear Bryant ran things at places like Texas A&M with the famed "Junction Boys."

Bryant's mentality was to beat your team into the ground, and only the strong will survive. "Coach Devaney had a way to make you want to play hard," said Jim Walden, who played under Devaney at Wyoming and later coached for him at Nebraska. "You got worked hard, but you didn't feel like you were being killed. It wasn't one of those boot camp mindset things. It was a let's get it done kind of a thing. We didn't practice every day. There wasn't a lot of time spent trying to see if we could take it or not. We didn't have that Bear Bryant reputation type thing. Coach Devaney just wanted you to work hard in the time we were out there. He'd scream at your ass, and you might have to start a couple of periods over, but going into the thing, we weren't out here on one of those Bataan marches. We were out here to learn to play, get better at football, and he brought that to us at Wyoming, and he took it to Nebraska. I'm sure—I wasn't there, but I can visibly see it—because we did it when I got to Nebraska in '69. My 1969 first practice in Nebraska reminded me so much of the same practice I had when I was in Wyoming playing for him. It didn't change much."

Devaney would get immediate results in his first season in 1962. His team won at Michigan 25–13. That got people's attention. They would lose to Missouri 16–7 and Big 8 champion Oklahoma 34–6 but eventually win the Gotham Bowl against Miami 36–34. It was NU's first bowl win in program history and the most wins they had in a season since going 10–0 in 1903. The Bob Devaney era was off and running.

Devaney was ahead of his time with not only how he structured his football practices, but also his approach with Black players in the 1950s and 1960s. The 1950s and 1960s were racially charged eras throughout the country, and that mentality spilled over to college athletics. Black football players were not the norm at major state universities. Devaney had a different outlook mainly because of how he was raised in Saginaw, Michigan.

Long before Devaney ever got into coaching, he was a boxer. There was a time in his life when Devaney thought he might go pro in the sport. "My dad grew up in basically a pretty tough section of Saginaw, and there were a lot of Black people that he was very good friends with," Mike Devaney said. "Back in those days, when you were a fighter, you were friends with Black people, too. He was as color blind as anybody I've ever known and never once had that thought in his mind at all. I can remember that even when we were in Michigan State there was a couple of Black players that used to babysit for my sister and I when they would go out. He never had any inklings or anything like that. I can remember being at Wyoming, and the guy that was the president of Wyoming was from the South. Wyoming was a little bit more segregated than I think Nebraska was. They were more on the south side of things. He was going to bring in the first Black athlete that they ever had there and talked to the president about it. The president said, 'Oh, Bob, I don't know if that's a good idea' and all this kind of stuff.

"My dad said, 'This is a good kid. I'll vouch for him. He'll come in here, and I'm sure he'll be a good citizen.' He finally talked the president into allowing him to do it. The kid came in, and during the spring game—or after he was in practice for a few days—they had some scrimmages, and the kid had some big plays.

"The president came up to my dad and said, 'You know, Bobby, that's the best-looking Hawaiian kid I've ever seen.'"

Walden also had fond memories of that story from Wyoming and of Devaney. "There's two things about him, and people need to know. He recruited one of the first Black athletes in the history of college football in a running back from Laramie, Wyoming. He was really a good player," Walden said. "He quit. I never did understand it. I didn't push it while I was there. It wasn't on bad terms. I think he just didn't want to play ball. He was a high school Black athlete, a really good player, a scholarship-deserving athlete from Laramie High if I'm not mistaken [in 1960]...Bob Devaney hired Bill Thornton in 1969 as a full-time staff member because I took his place when he left and went to California. He'd been there three years. I don't know how many Division I football programs or anybody had a full-time Black coach at that time in 1969, but Bob Devaney did."

There were also some interesting encounters when Nebraska played bowl games in places like Miami (1964) and New Orleans

(1967). According to former NU media relations director Don "Fox" Bryant, Auburn had never faced a Black player before the 1964 Orange Bowl. A lot of tension heading into the game even spilled over to NU's team hotel in Miami Beach. "We were staying at the Ivanhoe Hotel right there on the beach," former 1963 season assistant coach and eventual Nebraska head coach Tom Osborne recalled. "Joe Garagiola was one of the owners, the former pro baseball player. Bob, just said, 'If Black players can't stay here, then nobody's staying here.' They changed it."

A similar thing happened before the 1967 Sugar Bowl game against Alabama. Bryant's Crimson Tide would not have a Black player see the field in its program's history until 1971.

Some feel Devaney's 38–6 stomping of Alabama in the 1972 Orange Bowl and a 42–21 loss to USC in 1970 helped influence Bryant to break the color barrier in his program. Devaney and Trojans head coach John McKay featured several Black stand-out players in their programs. "I can remember there was a big instance at the 1967 Sugar Bowl when they were there, and one of the players was married to a white girl—a Black player was—and they were not going to let them stay at the hotel," Mike Devaney said. "Then, finally, they argued and they were going to make arrangements for him to go up the backstairs and all this other crap. My dad said, 'Listen, if he doesn't stay here, none of us are staying here,' and they were going to change hotels."

* * *

The memories of Bob Devaney at Nebraska are about so much more than winning national championships in 1970 and 1971. Devaney had a personality that could light up a room. He always found the party and could blend into any room. "I had one of the guys that I have known that used to be a supporter way back at that point in time," Mike Devaney said. "He said that my dad could walk into a room, spend the evening there with 150 people, and every one of them felt like they had a personal conversation with him. I think that back in those days, everybody worked hard, but they played hard, and they enjoyed life, too. Of course, I'm glad there were no cameras back in those days because I think that destroys the spontaneity that a lot of them had back in that time."

Jim Walden said he had never met a person like Devaney. He was the perfect combination in his era of college football. His ability to connect with coaches, players, and fans was rare. "He had a tremendous sense of humor," Walden said. "Not only was it a good public sense of humor in terms of being a good after-dinner speaker, if you want to use that term, he had a good wit about him, but he also carried that over to his players. He always had a real witty thing to be able to come back, a gleam in his eye about the way he could say something to you and yet slash that. He was tremendously competitive. You didn't fear him...because that same wit could turn into unbelievable verbiage—he could skin you alive, we used to say. He was very complex but fun. You didn't want to get on his bad side. You enjoyed too much the good side of Bob Devaney. I liked him. He knew how to talk to coaches."

One of those players, though, who managed to get on the bad side of Devaney was 1970 All-American linebacker Jerry Murtaugh. The Omaha North product nearly went to Oklahoma after the Sooners promised a car, plane tickets, and cash. Devaney caught wind of that and threatened to turn Murtaugh into the NCAA if he picked OU. The two had a love/hate relationship. Murtaugh was even kicked off the team for a day after an incident before the 1969 Sun Bowl in El Paso, Texas. A group of players got into trouble in nearby Juárez, Mexico, and Murtaugh was in the middle of it. Devaney was hot. Murtaugh rounded up cash to bail out a group of players who got arrested and appeared before a Mexican judge who asked him how much money he had. "I pulled it out and I said, 'I've got this.'"

Then Murtaugh nearly got arrested once police found four switchblade knives on him that he planned to take back to Nebraska. "I forgot I had bought four switchblades with pearl handles, and they were neater than hell," Murtaugh said. "I said, 'I'm going to take them back for my brothers.' But of course, they took them from me and they put them up on the desk, and I'm watching them. It's all next to the money. The interpreter comes over and yells at me, 'You dumb ass.'"

Finally, after everything was sorted out, one person was waiting for the group of players as they arrived back to their hotel in El Paso. "I got off the bus, and Devaney just unloaded on me, 'You did this. You got into...' We started screaming," Murtaugh said. "I said, 'I'm the guy that got them out of jail and I'm in all this shit.'

"He said, 'You're all off the team.' Everybody goes to their rooms, and they're calling each other.

"I said, 'Guys, he's not going to kick us off. We're all starters. Don't worry about it. He'll handle us after the game. He's got to win.'

"The next morning, we have a meeting with Devaney, and he's looking at everybody, and he said, 'You're lucky I don't kick you off right now.' I started laughing. Oh, he turned to me and said, 'You son of a bitch.'

"I just went, 'Oh, shit, I shouldn't laugh.'

"He said, 'You're all off the team after the game.' That's when I started laughing. We had a hell of a game. Then, that fall camp, he made us run extra, but he got the win. That's how that went in Juárez. That is the truth."

The tension with Devaney and Murtaugh didn't go away either. The two were very similar. Eventually, it was Phyllis Devaney, the wife of Bob, who finally got him and Murtaugh to speak years later. "Him and I had never sat down and talked to each other, but his retirement party, his wife called me and said, 'I want you at his retirement party,'

"I said, 'No, I'm not going.'

"She said, 'I will drive to Omaha and I will pick your ass up and I'll make you go.' She was a great lady.

"I said, 'For you, Mrs. Devaney, I'll be there.' We get there. I'm on one end; Devaney is on the other. His wife finds me. She comes up behind me and grabs me by my ear and starts tearing it. I stood up, and it was her. This little, tiny lady still had me by my ear and dragging me across the hall. Everybody is screaming, going nuts because I'm bent over sideways, and she's got my ear. Devaney is at the bar all by himself with nobody around him. She brought me up. She said, 'Sit down.' She looked at him, looked at me: 'Talk. I want you to talk.' She left, we sat there, not a word was said for about a minute.

"He looked at me and says, 'You want a beer?'

"I go, 'Yes.'

"We had a beer, and he said, 'Murtaugh, I want to tell you one thing: everybody thinks I'm a great football coach. They got it wrong. The one great thing I did, I hired the eight greatest assistants in the country. That I did do and I'll remember that.' He got up, walked away. We never said a word. He was smart; that's what he did. He hired the eight greatest assistants in the country."

Back in Devaney's day, college football coaching salaries were nowhere near what they are today. According to his son, Mike, the most Devaney ever made at Nebraska was $85,000.

However, a little-known story Mike Devaney shared from 1965 might have been one of the best financial offers a coach has ever received. After taking Nebraska to the Gotham, Orange, and Cotton Bowls in his first three seasons at NU, Devaney had several other people wanting to talk to him about coaching jobs, including at the pro level.

The way NU thanked Devaney for his loyalty was a group of boosters offered to buy him $50,000 in stock. The average price of a home in 1965 was around $21,500. Devaney had two options for the stock deal: American Food Host and a little-known stock called Berkshire Hathaway. He chose American Food Host over Berkshire Hathaway, which was valued at around $20 a share in 1965. It's now worth over $600,000 per share. He had the chance to own around 2,500 shares of it, which would be over $1 billion today. "That was in 1965. You can do the calculation, but it would have been a lot of money," Mike Devaney said, laughing. "If they'd picked [Berkshire], I don't think his salary would have mattered."

3

Frank Solich

IT WAS THE FALL OF 1966. FRANK SOLICH FINISHED AN
All-Big 8 career at Nebraska as a 5'7", 153-pound fullback. In
1965 he was the first ever Nebraska football player featured on
the cover of *Sports Illustrated* along with the first to rush for
more than 200 yards in a game.

Solich probably could've done whatever he wanted when his
playing career ended. He was a part of Bob Devaney's first recruiting class at NU that helped turn around the program, as the
Huskers played in two Orange Bowls and one Cotton Bowl during
Solich's final three seasons. Before Devaney got to Nebraska, NU
had played in just two bowl games in school history.

When Solich's career was over, he followed his heart. The
Pennsylvania native wanted to get into teaching and coaching.
He landed his first job at Holy Name High School in North
Omaha, Nebraska, at 22. It was a rebuilding job in some ways—
just like what Devaney walked into at Nebraska in 1962.

Solich was eager for the opportunity at Holy Name. "They got ahold of me and asked me to come up to Omaha, which I did," Solich said. "It wasn't really much of an interview, it didn't seem like. I took the job and I never looked back. I just felt that that would be a good start for me in terms of getting into coaching. I never told myself, 'Hey, you're going to be a pro coach,' or, 'You're going to be a head coach at Nebraska' or anything of that nature. I lived it day by day. I was looking forward to getting to Holy Name, getting started, and it ended up being just a great deal—only for two years. I loved it and to this day still have some players from Holy Name that get ahold of me, and we had a little bit of a reunion with a few of them [in 2023]. When I got started with it, I just got attached to it and just felt like I was in the right profession right from the start, even though it was starting in what was a Class B school at that time. Class A was the highest in Nebraska, but I still loved it and enjoyed it. I think it was a great, great start for me."

And like any small school job, Solich was more than just a football coach. Holy Name didn't have a stadium. They played their games at nearby Omaha Benson High School and practiced at Lake James Park at 48th and Bedford Ave. Besides his football position, Solich was also an assistant basketball coach. He loved everything about his new job. Most importantly, he was passionate about teaching and mentoring young football players. "Having played the game, I had a pretty good idea of what I wanted to be about in terms of how to set practices up from my high school days to my time at Holy Name," Solich said. "I grew into the job more or less and I had no experience obviously, as it was my first game and my first coaching opportunity. There was a guy there named Frank Spenceri, who was the head basketball coach and assistant football coach. I leaned on him and another coach, and they were there prior to me.

Obviously, you don't have much of a chance to hire your own staff in a Class B program like that. Those guys were very beneficial to me in organization and also relaying some thoughts about players to me."

The job presented some challenges early on, but Solich had Holy Name rolling by his second season. People were starting to take notice of the 23-year-old head coach in 1967. "We had to cross a major street and walk down to a park where we had practice," Solich said. "I had study hall duty, lunch duty—all those kinds of things added on to what else you do. That was typical. I think that's the way it is in most of those schools... That was no problem for me. I just looked forward to my time there and to see what I could do with the program. It was not flourishing at that time. I think our first season, we maybe won two games, and the next season, I think we were 8–2."

After the 1967 season, a unique opportunity came his way. Class A power Lincoln Southeast had a head football coach job opening. Solich loved everything about Holy Name, but this was a chance to get back to Lincoln, Nebraska, and coach a Class A power before age 25. "The position opened up. I stayed in touch with some of the Nebraska coaches, and as I talked to them, one of them said, 'Hey, you ought to get down here, get close to us, the position is open at Southeast.' I ended up doing that, went down for the interview," Solich said. "It was not an extensive interview, and I was able to get the job without having to put in much work to get it done. That was the start of my career there, and it ended up I was there 11 years. I really liked it and I was all set to stay. I really loved high school coaching."

Like at his job at Holy Name, Solich was much more than a football coach. He was involved in coaching in all three sports seasons, taught driver's ed, and was a part of an outdoor painting crew in the summer. "My right hip is still a little bothersome from using that brake on your side as the driver's ed instructor," Solich said, laughing. "All in all, that's what I did for many years there at Southeast. I was assistant swimming coach, assistant wrestling coach. Never was a swimming coach before. Never was a swimmer or never swam competitively and never wrestled competitively, but I was an assistant at both of those sports. I was a painter. We had a crew that got assignments. We went out and got jobs in Lincoln, painted houses, mostly outdoors, and that was my summer job."

During his 11 seasons at Southeast, Solich was 66–33–5. The Knights captured the Class A state championship during Solich's last two seasons, beating Omaha Creighton Prep in back-to-back finals. Then, 1975 was the first season the NSAA introduced a state football playoff system. Solich captured two of the first three Class A titles in state history.

Meanwhile, his former assistant coach at Nebraska, Tom Osborne, had recently replaced Devaney in 1973. By 1977 he had staff turnover and wanted to add new coaches. He reached out to Solich with an opportunity. "I'm not one that looks down the road in terms of a position and advancing and doing this. I just take care of the job I got. I always did as an assistant coach, as a head coach. I could've lived out my career being a high school coach with no problem and would've enjoyed that as a career," Solich said. "Obviously, getting the chance to start out at the University of Nebraska and being under Tom Osborne was something that was pretty special."

Solich still recalls when the phone call came from Osborne with the offer. "Coach Osborne was at a convention or a speaking engagement," Solich said. "He had called me and talked to me about a position that was opening up. It was the head freshman coach, which is a part-time coaching position. Back in those days, Nebraska had a freshman team, and they'd go around playing a lot of some third-team guys or second-team guys from other schools, guys that weren't getting a lot of playing time at some schools. We would take our freshman team and go play them, maybe a junior college or two. It was a great start for me on the college level."

Regarding pay, it may have been a step down from what Solich was making at Lincoln Southeast. It was never about the money, though. When you find something that you are passionate about, the money is secondary. "Neither one I think was great pay. I think high school might've been a little more, but I'm not sure exactly what the amounts were," Solich said. "Again, that was not something that bothered me much. If it seemed like the right thing to do, then the pay wouldn't have mattered all that much. I hate to sound ridiculous with that, but that's how I am. It wouldn't have made a difference if I was getting more money at the high school level than I'd got as a freshman coach. That wouldn't have played into my decision whatsoever."

After four years serving as Osborne's freshman coach, Solich became the running backs coach in 1983. Talk about timing. Solich stepped into the role during the peak of the "Scoring Explosion" offense that featured quarterback Turner Gill, running back Mike Rozier, and wide receiver Irving Fryar. Under Solich's tutelage, Rozier would go on to win the 1983 Heisman Trophy and he's still the program's only running back to rush for more than 2,000 yards in a season.

People were starting to take notice of Solich. He was regarded as the best running backs coach in the country. Solich was also learning under one of the best of all time in Osborne. "There were a lot of good football players on those teams," Solich said. "Coach Osborne and Coach Devaney were as good as it gets in terms of coaching and handling young men, but, of course, Coach Osborne was special. I think he probably could've coached at any position on the team. It was clear when we had meetings that he just didn't attend the meetings that some head coaches do and just make sure things are going well and let maybe the coordinators really totally run with it. He was skilled in every way when it came to coaching—from the different positions to how he handled young men to how he handled his coaches."

By 1992 things were just starting to get going for Osborne in Lincoln. However, former Huskers player and Wisconsin head coach Barry Alvarez was beginning to turn a corner at Wisconsin. He was interested in talking to Solich. Nobody knew what Osborne's long-term plan was. Osborne was the head coach and offensive coordinator, so there were not many advancement opportunities for Solich. The defensive-minded Alvarez offered Solich his offensive coordinator job in 1992. That was enough to get Osborne's attention and let Solich in on his long-term plan.

It was similar when Texas Tech pursued Osborne as their head coach, leading to Devaney to tab him as his successor. Osborne did something just like that with Solich. He wanted Solich to be his successor. He told Solich his plan was to coach until the 1996 season and added assistant head coach to Solich's title. "In 1992 Barry Alvarez tried to hire him as an offensive coordinator," Osborne said. "I told Frank, 'I think I'll go five more years and I'd like to have you take over.' Five years came and went, and then we were going into the 1997 season, and Grant Wistrom and Jason Peter were guys who were pretty much consensus first-round draft picks. They were juniors. They came in to see me, and I thought they were going to tell me they were going to go into the NFL. They said, 'We're 9–2 this year.'

"I said, 'Yes, I knew that.'

"They said, 'Well, we didn't think that was very good.'

"I said, 'Yes, I agree.'

"They said, 'We're going to come back.'

"I told Frank, I said, 'I feel a little awkward taking off with these guys coming back.' He agreed that I'd go one more year. Of course, we ended up winning it all, but we were a little lucky down in Missouri."

What a dream scenario at least on paper. Solich stepped in during the 1998 season after the Huskers just came off a historic 60–3 five-year run, winning three national championships.

However, as they say, you never want to be the coach who follows a legend. Osborne himself experienced that in his own right. The only difference was that legend, Devaney, was his athletic director. Solich's two athletic directors he worked for had nothing to do with his hiring. "In his first year, I think he had a lot of injuries that were pretty crippling. I think he went 9–4," Osborne said. "Then the next year, he could have won the title, and I think they fumbled down at Texas. Otherwise, they might have had an undefeated season. Then he played for a national championship and he won a conference championship. Then he had that one year where they were 7–7. In his last year, he was 9–3. Overall, he won 75 percent of his games. There aren't very many people in the College Football Hall of Fame that have won 75 percent of their games."

But Solich was fired in 2003. "When that decision was made it was something I felt very strongly about. I didn't hear about it until after it was made," Osborne said. "I got phone messages. I was out of town somewhere and had a couple of phone messages that Frank had been fired, but that was after the fact. I felt very bad about that. Then [Steve Pederson] had a long pursuit for the new coach. I think maybe [Pederson] had different people in mind, and that didn't work out, and then Bill Callahan was hired. Anyway, the rest is history."

When Osborne named Solich his successor, it was a different time. In 1997 Osborne was the king of college football. There was no search committee or opinion from athletic director Bill Byrne. Osborne simply told Byrne the plan for the program with Solich. "A lot of times ADs like to hire their own person," Osborne said. "I don't know quite what Bill's reaction was, but I think he felt the tea leaves were such that he'd need to go along with it. I can't say any more than that."

The other thing Osborne wanted to keep was continuity. He feared that if he turned the process over to Byrne, an entirely new coaching staff might have been at Nebraska by 1998.

"Frank had been made the assistant head coach. He had that title. We'd had a lot of success," Osborne said. "The question here was: why would you bring somebody in and lose the whole staff? The thing I was concerned about was all the coaches because I imagine most of them would have been gone. I felt a certain loyalty to those guys, too. Now, if I'd been told that if I quit, that they're going to start over, I probably would have stayed on, but as long as Frank could be the coach, there would be continuity. I felt that was what I needed to do at that point."

What Osborne did not know was what would play out in 2002. NU had just finished a 7–6 regular season. Solich was forced to make some staff changes and hired six new assistant coaches. During that time Byrne was being courted by Texas A&M for their athletic director opening. Byrne ended up leaving for College Station, Texas. A few weeks later, Nebraska named Pederson, a North Platte, Nebraska, native as athletic director. He came to NU from Pittsburgh, where he was their athletic director.

This was arguably one of the turning points of Nebraska football history. Pederson and Solich did not have a great relationship, dating back to when he served as Osborne's recruiting coordinator. When Solich hired six new assistant coaches for the 2003 season, immediately the staff knew they were on thin ice with Pederson. Solich had verbally offered them standard two-year assistant coach agreements. The contracts the coaches got read differently. Pederson attempted to change the language in the deals to say they would stop getting paid when there was any type of head coaching change at Nebraska. That's unheard of in major college football with assistant coaches.

After beating Colorado in Boulder and finishing 9–3 in 2003, the staff thought they might be safe. Former offensive coordinator Barney Cotton still had his doubts. Only a week before that win in Boulder, the *Lincoln Journal Star* reported through anonymous sources that Pederson would fire Solich at season's end. Cotton knew things were not on solid ground with Solich and Pederson, and that's exactly how it played out. Imagine winning a game on ABC to finish 9–3 and then being fired later that evening when the team returned to Lincoln. "Frank put together a staff that he thought could be a staff for the long haul, and obviously it didn't work that way," Cotton said. "I was probably one of the few that after we beat Colorado—guys are hooting and hollering, and we had a good finish to the season—I didn't have a good feeling about it because I knew our leadership wasn't fully behind us. I didn't have a good feeling about it in the locker room. Guys said afterward, 'We're okay.'

"And I said, 'You know what, guys? I'm not sure we are.' A number of them thought I was wrong obviously, but my gut told me things. It wasn't sitting right with me the way that the leadership at that point was treating us, I can say it that way...I was eating dinner with my wife and three boys and I got the phone call like at 6:00 or 7:00 at night."

Pederson's criticism of Solich was he could not recruit at a level to compete with new Big 12 hotshots Texas and Oklahoma. They were led by head coaches Mack Brown and Bob Stoops, respectively, and both became national powers. Stoops won a national title at OU in 2000, while Brown later won one at Texas in 2005. "They tried to say Frank could not recruit. How many draft choices were on that team?" Cotton said. Solich's final roster in 2003 produced 17 eventual NFL draft picks. "You had [Richie] Incognito and [Josh] Sewell and Cory Ross and others on offense. What, did we have 10 that year, maybe six or seven on defense? We had first rounders, second rounders. That was a talented bunch, though. They forced 45 turnovers that year or something like that. You had Barrett Ruud. Oh, my goodness. That is as talented of defense as anybody's got. That would rival—if you would look at draft choice-wise—that rivals almost any defense you see in the draft. It just drives me crazy to think that people say that the recruiting was one of the reasons why Frank got let go. That is absolute bullshit when you look at those teams. That was in his sixth year as a head coach."

Pederson was fired in 2007. Osborne would replace him as athletic director and eventually fire Callahan. When Osborne reflects on Pederson's time at NU, his downfall is that he wasn't a true football guy. "I ran into [Pederson] once or twice [after his firing]. I've never been an enemy of Steve," Osborne said. "Steve worked for me and did a good job. I don't have any bad feelings toward Steve, but he had come at it from a different standpoint. He'd been a guy that had worked in recruiting and he had a lot of good ideas. He's a creative guy, but his background wasn't coaching, so he had a little different viewpoint."

* * *

After Frank Solich was fired by Nebraska in 2003, Army reached out to him to be their head coach. They thought they had him. A press release was already drafted. Solich ended up sitting out the 2004 season instead. He used the year to learn and watch other great coaches. He checked out the Tampa Bay Buccaneers to watch his former teammate Monte Kiffin. He stopped by USC to study how Pete Carroll was doing things. He also visited Mack Brown at Texas, Bob Stoops at Oklahoma, and Dick Vermeil with the Kansas City Chiefs to watch their coaching staffs in action.

By 2005 Solich was ready to step back in. Ohio had an opportunity. They were a bottom feeder in the Mid-American Conference and by no means considered an attractive job. In many ways, it was no different than the 22-year-old Solich taking over at Holy Name. He had his work cut out for him, but he had a process he believed in. He decided to build things in Athens, Ohio, with the same mindset he did in Lincoln, Nebraska.

One of the coaches who followed Solich to Ohio was Jimmy Burrow. The former Huskers defensive back was a graduate assistant under Solich when his oldest son, Jamie, played for the Big Red, as did his son Dan. He also had another notable son who spent the early years of his life around Nebraska football—2019 Heisman Trophy-winning quarterback Joe Burrow. "None of us really knew anything about Ohio football," Jimmy Burrow said. "Coach Solich had hired Tim Albin, and so they both put the full-court press on me to come from North Dakota State, where I was content working with Craig Bohl. I thought we were on the verge of doing some great things, which played out. They won some national championships over the years after that, but when I got here, nobody expected us to win. As a matter of fact, people around town said, 'Hey, we have a great band,' and so people said, 'Hey, your first job is to get people to stay past halftime' because people would come to the game, they'd hear the band, and then they would leave.

"People said, 'Your first goal is to get everybody to stay in the stands for the second half after the band plays.' The first home game was against Pittsburgh in overtime, and we upset them on national television. We kept them in the stands for pretty much the whole time we were here. Think about that: you're talking about respect that coaches have and think about Coach Solich coming to Ohio University, and our first home game was on ESPN against Pittsburgh on a Friday night. That's the respect that coach had earned while coaching at Nebraska, but there were challenges financially, getting players here, recruiting, getting our team to expect to win. Coach Solich just did a great job trusting Tim Albin and I to install the offense and defense. He also knew that what we were all ingrained in Nebraska, which was important. That's why Ross Els was hired who didn't play at Nebraska but grew up in Lincoln. Gerry Gdowski was hired, and Keven Lightner was hired because that was the type of culture. The culture that we had experienced at Nebraska was the type of culture that he wanted instill in our football team. I think that all helped it play out as it did."

Burrow was with Solich for 14 seasons at Ohio, while Albin was there all 16. The Bobcats won 115 games during Solich's 16 seasons. Albin succeeded Solich in 2021, while Burrow retired after the 2018 season so he could watch his son, Joe, play quarterback for LSU and then the Cincinnati Bengals.

If Solich's time at Ohio proved anything, it's that his way worked. He knew how to build a program, adapt, and mentor players and, most importantly, he had a staff that believed in him.

"Getting the Ohio University football program to where it is today is certainly one of his proudest accomplishments,"

Burrow said. "To be here that 14 years like I was and to see it, it's the transition, and his leadership was amazing. I was just fortunate to be a part of that. That was one of the reasons for those 14 years, I think I had two job interviews and I really didn't seek those jobs. I didn't send out resumes every year. I didn't think the grass was greener on the other side, so to speak. I'd coached at the Power Five level, and Coach Solich treated us all so well here as assistants. I got to go to almost every Friday night game that [my son] Joe played. If we were on a bus ride to Akron and Joe played here on Friday night—Jesse Williams was our D-line coach, and his son was the running back with Joe. He would let Jesse and I stay behind, watch the game, and then drive our car to Akron or wherever—he allowed us to have a family life, put it that way. You go, 'Why would I want to leave somebody that allows us to do things like that and treats us well as an assistant?' That's why I chose to be with him for 14 years.

"I'm not speaking for him, but I would say he had a chip on his shoulder when he came to Ohio University. He wanted to prove that he could change the program, and once we changed it, to continue to be successful. Once again, there are doubters when you get let go, right? Whether it's the president, whether it's the AD, whether it's the board and coaches, in some cases, the fans. I don't think with Coach Solich the fans were on board certainly with that. You're trying to prove that that was not a good decision. I think he did that very well."

* * *

When Tom Osborne took over as the athletic director and named Bo Pelini head coach in 2008, there were multiple attempts to get Frank Solich back to Nebraska. Osborne, Pelini, and Scott Frost all tried to make it happen. You have to give former athletic director Trev Alberts credit. His persistence got Solich back for the 2023 Red–White spring game weekend.

He was finally properly honored for the man he was. Solich, who was inducted into the College Football Hall of Fame in 2024, gave nearly his entire life to Nebraska football. Alberts hosted a reception for him that featured several notable coaches and players, including Osborne, Barry Alvarez, Kansas head coach Lance Leipold, and all three Nebraska Heisman Trophy winners.

During the spring game, he was honored on the field. When Matt Rhule was named head coach at Nebraska in November of 2022, one of the first things he did was reach out to Solich—the two crossed paths when Rhule coached at Temple in the MAC Conference. "They've been trying to get him back since Bo Pelini and that staff tried to get him back," Jimmy Burrow said. "Almost every staff did. Some of the staff members have reached out to me to try to encourage him, but I would always politely mention it, and he just wasn't ready. I think Trev Alberts made a concerted effort to reach out to Coach Solich. I think Coach Rhule, from what I understand, one of his first calls when he became head coach was to Coach Solich…Coach Osborne being there, I'm sure, has been a part of reaching out to him over the years and trying to get him to come back. He had to be ready because he was ready. Even a month or two before he committed to doing it, it wasn't a sure thing that he was going to agree to it. We had dinner with him, Pam [Solich], Coach Albin, and my wife. We encouraged him to do it and we felt it was time."

Solich's return to Nebraska won't erase any of the last 20-plus years of losses, but it did provide some closure. Over his coaching career, Solich was 173–101. He was 58–19 in six seasons at Nebraska. He won the school's last conference title, coached two Heisman Trophy winners, and took Nebraska to its last national championship game during the 2001 season. "I just felt comfortable with it right now," Solich said. "Coach Rhule, I know when he got to town, he got ahold of Coach Osborne and he texted me some, and we texted back and forth and talked on the phone maybe once or twice. That wasn't happening before. I just felt welcomed in that manner and I knew it would be good to get back and be a part of what Nebraska is all about. I looked forward to it and am glad I'm here. I've been invited back several times by Trev. He was relentless. He kept after it. It makes a lot of sense to be back. I spent a lot of time on that field out there. My family spent a lot of time here. We consider it our home. It's great to be back."

4

Bo Pelini

IN 2002 NEBRASKA FAILED TO WIN NINE GAMES AS A FOOTBALL program for the first time since 1968. The Huskers finished 7–7 and lost to Ole Miss in the Independence Bowl. This was on the heels of the 2001 season, where Miami blew the Big Red out in the Rose Bowl for the national championship. Frank Solich needed some fresh blood in the Huskers program. He needed to revamp his defensive staff. He parted ways with defensive coordinator Craig Bohl, defensive line coach Nelson Barnes, and secondary coach George Darlington. Offensive line coach Milt Tenopir and assistant offensive line coach Dan Young retired while running backs coach Dave Gillespie moved into an off-the-field role. The only assistants that stayed on after 2002 were quarterbacks coach Turner Gill, wide receivers coach Ron Brown, and defensive line coach Jeff Jamrog.

After a legendary career, Charlie McBride retired as Nebraska's defensive coordinator in 1999. Bohl was his handpicked successor, and things began to go downhill with his scheme and approach by the end of 2001. Solich needed some new ideas to build his defense around. Who did he go to when searching for advice on finding a new defensive coordinator? His former Huskers teammate Monte Kiffin. The Lexington, Nebraska, native just won Super Bowl XXXVII with the Tampa Bay Buccaneers. At that time he was regarded as the top defensive mind in the NFL, as his coaching staff featured names like Mike Tomlin. Pete Carroll also cut his teeth under Kiffin. Solich called Kiffin for a few recommendations and he then reached out to Carroll, who was very early in his tenure at USC. "I said, 'Pete, who's out there right now in college football that would be a really, really good coordinator at Nebraska?'" Kiffin said. "I told him, 'I'm trying to help out Frankie Solich.'

"And he told me, 'There are a lot of good college coaches out there, but I'll give you a guy that might just go back to college football, and that's Bo Pelini [who was a Green Bay Packers linebacker coach at the time but previously had worked for Carroll]. Let me call Bo and see if he'd have some interest.' Pete called Bo, and Bo called Pete back, and they talked, and then Pete called me back, and then I called Bo, and then I called Frank. That's how one thing led to another."

It was that moment that brought Pelini into the Huskers family. Solich hired Pelini as his defensive coordinator. The other five hires he made had either played at Nebraska in their career or had previously been a part of the program. The Pelini hire was completely out of the box, but in the end, it would be a home run. Barney Cotton was named Solich's offensive coordinator in 2003.

Solich conducted nearly all his new staff hires at the AFCA Convention in New Orleans. Cotton said he immediately felt good about Pelini the first time they talked. "The first time I met Bo was in that room at New Orleans when he was the defensive coordinator, and he was sitting at the table," Cotton said. "It was a big conference table in a Marriott, and that's the first time I met him, and then little by little, we got to be not just coaching mates. We became good friends. We could talk about football. It was a good relationship. Bo was really sharp. The thing I always liked to do—and I don't know if everybody did—I like to talk to d-coordinators about what we did and if we did this, what would you do, back and forth, and stuff like that...because defensive guys obviously know defense better than offensive guys do. Offensive guys may give defensive guys a different perspective because I remember Bo coming in as well and saying, 'This is what they do. If we did this, what would you do?'"

Carroll also spoke glowingly about his former protege Pelini. "We've been together a long time, and I watched him kind of grow up in coaching," Carroll said in 2008. "He's got a great sense for what's happening and he's a very bright, tough guy. He's a really demanding coach that's innovative. He's really got all the right stuff and he's a great competitor, and that comes through in his style of coaching."

The spring of 2003 was challenging for Solich, as he had to work with nearly an entire new staff. He also had a new boss in athletic director Steve Pederson.

Former Huskers and new secondary coach Marvin Sanders remembers Pelini's first ever game as defensive coordinator against Oklahoma State. The contest was moved up to Week One for national television. The Cowboys had just beaten the Huskers in 2002, tearing down the goalposts in Stillwater, Oklahoma. It was their first win over NU since 1961. They were led by new head coach Les Miles and his hotshot offensive coordinator Mike Gundy. OSU was ranked No. 24 coming into Lincoln and picked by everyone to win the game.

The problem was that Oklahoma State had no idea what Pelini's defense would look like. It was his first ever game as defensive coordinator. They studied a lot of Green Bay film since Pelini had worked there under defensive coordinator Ed Donatell. Instead, Pelini came out in more of a Tampa 2 defense that OSU did little to no prep work for. Gundy's offense looked lost. Pelini's defense flew around that Saturday as 800 former Huskers players watched from the sideline. The Cowboys offense only had 183 yards, including just 57 yards in the second half. Pelini's new-look Blackshirt defense forced five turnovers, and Oklahoma State's All-American wide receiver Rashaun Woods had just five catches for 47 yards, his lowest output in 15 games.

It was like Pelini came into Lincoln and waved a magic wand. Husker Nation was immediately captivated. "There was something on ESPN that showed how heavy favored Oklahoma State was," Sanders said. "I'm like, 'How are they [a] big favorite? We're in Nebraska.' We had a rough season [in 2002], but we're still in Nebraska. I remember Bo not being happy about that. Our players weren't happy about it. I think they really came out and played at a high level. That was a little bit of motivation thanks to the picks by ESPN."

In just one year, Pelini took Nebraska's struggling defense from being ranked 55th nationally in 2002 to leading the nation in turnover margin and being ranked 11th in 2003. Pelini suddenly became one of the hottest young coaches in college football. His connection to Bob Stoops and Youngstown (Ohio) Cardinal Mooney also grabbed people's attention. In 2003 Stoops was regarded as one of the top coaches in college football.

In the end none of it mattered. Pederson fired Solich after a 9–3 regular season in 2003. It was a decision many felt Pederson pre-determined once the Huskers lost to both Kansas State and Missouri. He was never going to bring back Solich. The newly-hired six assistant coaches soon realized that in the summer of 2003. "There was some changing in the language of the contracts that Frank had told me we would get, and we didn't get them until July," Sanders said. "When that language was changed, we made a joke that anything outside of a championship we probably wouldn't be here based on the language in the contract. Coach Cotton had brought it to my attention, but it wasn't the extra year. It was [that] our contracts would've ended the day that Frank failed to occupy the position of a head coach for any reason. That raised a little suspicion, but again, I'm thinking, *We're at Nebraska, we're home, we got to perform is what's expected.* We thought we'd have more time."

The decision to fire Solich strengthened Pelini's name more. He was named the interim head coach for the Alamo Bowl, and after multiple national candidates for the job had turned down Pederson, the cries for Pelini to replace Solich began to get louder. Pelini's team played inspired football in San Antonio, winning the Alamo Bowl against Michigan State 17–3. Chants of "We want Bo!" took over the Alamodome as Pelini thanked the sold-out crowd of Huskers fans on the microphone. Pederson eventually turned the page. After a 41-day coaching search, he hired Bill Callahan.

Pelini took a job at Oklahoma to work under Bob Stoops, Mike Stoops, and Brent Venables. He eventually left OU to become Miles' defensive coordinator at LSU in 2005. In 2007 LSU captured the national championship.

* * *

Just like in 2003, Nebraska was searching for a defensive-minded coach in 2008. Tom Osborne fired Bill Callahan following a 5–7 season in 2007, where Nebraska had some of the worst defensive numbers in program history. NU gave up 76 points to Kansas and 65 points to Colorado during the 2007 season. They edged out Ball State 41–40 earlier in the year. These were unheard-of numbers for Nebraska football. In October of 2007, Osborne took over as athletic director after Steve Pederson was relieved of his duties by chancellor Harvey Perlman.

Things had fallen off the tracks, and Osborne knew the program needed a strong defensive coach. Osborne reportedly interviewed Bo Pelini, Turner Gill, Navy's Paul Johnson, and Wake Forest's Jim Grobe, among others. "Bo Pelini had been here and had a fair amount of support among the players," Osborne said. "He seemed to be a good defensive coach, and that's really where we were struggling. I remember we played down at Kansas under Bill Callahan, and Kansas hung 76 points on us, and we just couldn't stop anybody, and so Bo wasn't the only guy I talked to, but of the available candidates, the way it shook out, not everybody was interested in the job. I thought he was probably the best option. I'm not trying to necessarily stick up for Bo, but he won nine or 10 games every year, and players liked him. The players' graduation rate was really good, good discipline, but his interaction with the public and the press was rocky. That eventually, I guess, did him in, but a lot of people would think back and think *nine or 10 wins a year*, it's not too bad, but it just is what it is."

Pelini brought a no-nonsense approach back to Nebraska football. He ran it like a college program. He emphasized the importance of academics so much that he would check campus lecture halls himself to ensure players attended class. He didn't want guys out at the bar scene either and he had an interesting approach to make sure that didn't happen. "Bo was like, 'Hey, I don't want anybody going on O Street after a game.' We were like, 'Okay, that's fine. We totally get it, we understand where you're coming from.' I was like, 'We'll make that rule,'" former 2008 starting quarterback Joe Ganz said. "My friends that weren't part of football were out at The Rail or The Bar. They were all out there. They would tell me like, 'Yes, Bo came into The Rail and was looking around, and everyone was chanting his name and shit. It was awesome.' It was: he wasn't doing it for that aspect of it. He was doing the: hey, we made this rule, we're going to enforce it. I know the student body guys—that weren't involved in the football program at all—they thought it was awesome. They loved it, and The Rail had even named a drink after Carl [Pelini] and all that. They just loved it. That was just Bo. He just did things out of the blue, what he thought was right for everybody in the program, and it turned out that people really enjoyed it or turned it into something fun, and he had nothing but really good intentions about it."

Pelini also proved to be a pretty good football coach. His teams always won nine or 10 games as Osborne stated. They played in three conference title games over seven years. His defenses were regarded as some of the best in the country, especially in 2009 and 2010, where the Huskers featured multiple high-level NFL players. Defensive lineman Ndamukong Suh finished his career under Pelini in 2009 as the most decorated defensive player in program history. And cornerback Prince Amukamara remains NU's most recent first-round draft pick, and that occurred in 2011. "One of the things that made [Pelini] so special was he was exceptionally intelligent, and he could see the game almost from a different perspective," former defensive coordinator John Papuchis said. "He was one move ahead of most everybody we were playing against in terms of the chess match. He had a great ability to anticipate during the course of the week what we would see and have a plan for it. Even if it hadn't showed itself on film yet to be an issue, he could foresee things that potentially could be things that would show up down the road and already have a plan of what he would do next. I think he had a phenomenal mind when it came to being creative and how we would be able to match routes. I think a reflection of his intelligence was his memory, and the way he could remember things off the film and how routes were run was exceptional. I think for that time period where we were together, both at LSU and Nebraska, I was always so impressed about just the way his mind worked and the way he was creative but always thoughtful in how he approached the game."

As we later learned, Pelini's demise at Nebraska had nothing to do with wins and losses.

Pelini fell victim to a university political hierarchy that did not want him there. Osborne hired Pelini under Perlman's watch. Osborne also bailed out Perlman after Pederson was fired in 2007. In 2010 Osborne played a significant hand in helping get the Huskers into the Big Ten. Once Perlman had the move to the Big Ten in place, it became clear he did not want Pelini representing the University of Nebraska.

Things came to a boiling point in 2010 at Texas A&M when the Huskers lost 9–6. NU had a school-record 16 penalties, and the Aggies had just two. The loss cost the Huskers a possible BCS at-large bid, which would've lowered Nebraska's overall exit fee payout to the Big 12. Pelini completely melted down that night in College Station, Texas. Perlman called him out the next day to the Associated Press. That was the first shot fired.

By 2012 Osborne was reportedly forced to retire by Perlman. A few weeks later, he named Shawn Eichorst Nebraska's next AD after promising Osborne he could have a hand in the process. In fact, Osborne had multiple candidates he had promised would get an interview for the job. Instead, Perlman conducted his own private search with the assistance of Wisconsin athletic director Barry Alvarez, who turned him on to Eichorst at Miami. "When [Osborne] went away, there was a change in the air. That's for sure," former defensive line coach Rick Kaczenski said. "There wasn't the comfort level that we definitely had with T.O."

Pelini's brash style finally caught up with him. When Eichorst was hired, it became evident that his main job was to hire a new football coach. He kept his distance from Pelini and the football program. He had a very corporate style as athletic director that didn't work well at Nebraska. There were several layers of management between Eichorst and the coaches. He was impossible to meet with.

Eichorst fired Pelini following the 2014 season after the Huskers won nine games and beat Iowa. Pelini addressed his team at a secret meeting at Lincoln North Star High School after being fired. "[I] appreciate you guys coming out, and obviously the last couple days for me have been kind of crazy, just giving you guys a heads up it wasn't a surprise to me. It really wasn't," Pelini said, as audio from the meeting later leaked out on the Internet. "Since I've been here, [Eichorst] has been here for two years. I've had a conversation with the guy a couple of times. You've seen him. He's never been in the locker room and at the end of the day he was never going to support us. And he didn't support us, and you saw it."

Once Osborne retired in 2012, that impacted Pelini and how he acted daily. Eichorst's approach to Pelini put him on an island, and that pressure eventually drove him over the edge.

"He's a little bit of a loner in some ways," Osborne said of Pelini. "I can't say we're enemies. I think I got along with him. I think if things got rocky, I could always visit with him, and things would settle down. When I left I think [Eichorst] eventually wouldn't have anything to do with him or had very little, let's put it that way. As a result, I think things got worse."

And as former Huskers running back Tony Davis said, Pelini was the type that couldn't handle that, and it eventually cost him. "I love Bo as a coach," Davis said. "Bo is a good coach."

Davis, though, noted when Steve Sipple from the *Lincoln Journal Star* called him asking about Pelini. "I said, 'Listen, he will not lose a job because he can't coach,'" Davis said. "'He'll lose his job because he can't get along with people.'"

There was another side of Pelini that very few people saw. He was unique in a lot of ways. He took his kids to school every morning. He rarely missed any of their sporting events. He always found time for his family despite his busy schedule. Pelini never missed Sunday mass, often occupying the back row of St. Peter's Catholic Church in Lincoln. It wasn't uncommon to see Pelini jogging across campus even on gamedays. When the Huskers played at night, Pelini liked to run through downtown Lincoln to burn off some steam. And his runs weren't just light jogs. They were typically high-level pushes that carried the same type of Pelini intensity he was known for.

Pelini was also very generous with his time to local charities and schools, including Lincoln Pius X High School and the University of Nebraska's Newman Center (St. Thomas Aquinas Catholic Church). One of the things he did for Pius X was help purchase field turf for their football stadium. At the Newman Center, he played a significant role in purchasing three alters from Immaculate Conception Catholic Church in Pelini's hometown of Youngstown, Ohio. The Newman Center was a $25 million project.

Father Robert Matya from St. Thomas Aquinas was a regular around the program. Matya was on the sidelines and said a catholic mass before games. The university leadership did not support Matya being part of the NU traveling party. So Pelini paid for Father Matya's trips out of his pocket once the university said he could no longer have accommodations on road trips. If a graduate assistant or younger coach was having financial struggles, Pelini was always the first guy there to help.

Pelini had a very giving side, which is one of the reasons why coaches and players were so loyal to him. "The thing about him is his best deeds were always unseen," Papuchis said. "There was a lot of things that were seen that people passed judgment on, but the greatest things he did for people, including for myself, were things that nobody knows about. To me, those are the real good people that don't do good just so they can show everyone how much good they're doing, but they do good because they feel like it's the right thing to do."

For as demanding as Pelini appeared to be on Saturdays, he was a great head coach to work for. He didn't believe in being at the office at 6:00 AM and working until midnight. He thought there should be balance in the program. When Pelini was fired in 2014, Cotton took over as interim head coach for the Holiday Bowl against USC. He remembers how badly the team wanted to honor Pelini in the bowl game. "The players, they really liked Bo," Cotton said. "A lot of people remember Bo as the guy with the temper and stuff like that. Bo's competitive side really came out on Saturday. If you said one thing about Bo Pelini, you would say how competitive that he was...He got a bad rep because you see a heck of a lot of coaches do things at least like what he did and possibly worse and not even get called out about it. Then they get called 'competitive.' They weren't put into the same microscope that Bo was. Bo was a good guy to work for in the office. He let you coach your players. Again, we had the same communication when he was the head coach that we did as assistant coaches and stuff like that. There was a lot of loyalty on that team from a coach's standpoint and a player standpoint. To the point: when I was the interim head coach, Bo hated team pictures.

"We had the team picture at the end of the year. Bo had been fired. Because for whatever reason—we had rain or something—the team picture didn't get taken, and so we never took it because Bo didn't want to take that time during the season or whatever at the end of preseason to take the picture. We're taking the picture in the auditorium in December, and the camera crew and Shawn Eichorst's crew is in there, and we're getting ready to take the picture. I'd looked at previous pictures, and so I had an empty seat, and that's where Bo would've been sitting at. The guys up front, they're saying, 'Hey, slide in, slide in. There's an empty seat right there, slide in.'

"I said, 'No, don't move.'

"They said, 'No, we got to slide in. There's an empty seat.'

"I said, 'No, that's not an empty seat. That's Bo's seat. We're going to take this picture and we're going to honor Bo by leaving that seat empty for him.' I don't even know if this picture ever came out because you can always edit pictures. We took our team picture with that seat in the middle for Bo, even though he wasn't there because that was truly his team."

Since being fired in 2014, Pelini's appearances in Nebraska have been next to none. However, the tragic death of offensive lineman Cole Pensick in April of 2023 brought Pelini back to the state. That's how much his players meant to him. Pensick was the first commit of Pelini's 2009 recruiting class. His father, Dan Pensick, was a former Husker and attended nearly every practice of his son's five-year career. Pelini's presence for the visitation and funeral was moving to many of his former players. Most importantly, it showed how much he still cared about them despite how his time ended at Nebraska. "He hung out with us Thursday night all night and then was there again on Friday for the funeral services and again just the testament to the person he was and the family man that he was," former fullback and 2009 recruit C.J. Zimmerer said of Pelini's time at Pensick's funeral services. "He treated all of us players like we were his kids. He was protective of us, would do anything for us, and that's proof right there in one gesture of him coming to a funeral."

5

Scott Frost

It was June 16, 2021. Scott Frost was coming off his third season at Nebraska with a 3–5 record. This after a 5–7 mark in 2019 and a 4–8 record in 2018. Frost and several members of the NU athletic department were taking part in a promotional Big Red Blitz caravan tour around the state. The day began in North Platte, Nebraska, with Frost speaking to around 120 fans in a gym at Mid-Plains Community College. His final stop on the tour was in Kearney at the Younes Conference Center, just 30 miles away from his hometown of Wood River.

This was supposed to be the anchor stop of the Big Red Blitz. The venue was set up with seating for more than 500 people, but a crowd of closer to 50 spaced out comfortably in the banquet hall that hosts several statewide conventions each year. Making up nearly half that number were several media members and employees from First National Bank—the presenting sponsor of the Big Red Blitz. "I've got to tell you: usually when

I'm up in front of people like this, there are many more people than this. This is kind of small and intimate," Frost told the crowd. "The first year that I signed at Nebraska and came back to coach, we went and did a couple of these things in Columbus and other places, and I think there was like 4,000 people there or something crazy. It tells me I better start winning. I'm starting to feel like the Charlie Daniels Band. He used to be really big and now he just plays county fairs."

Crowds were sparse all over the tour. You could blame the small turnout on several things. Maybe it was a lack of marketing or the fact that the event was held on a Wednesday at 2:30 PM. The bottom line was that things felt much different from when the native son was first announced as head coach in December 2017. Less than two weeks later, Frost's world would begin to change forever. Bill Moos, the athletic director who hired him, was forced out on June 25—coincidently shortly after his appearances on the Big Red Blitz in Alliance and Scottsbluff.

Then university chancellor Ronnie Green and president Ted Carter paid Moos nearly $3 million to go away. To this day, no exact reason has been given. Some have speculated that Moos' lack of oversight of the football program played a factor.

The 70-year-old Moos at that time also owned a ranch in Washington that he frequented several weeks a year, keeping himself at arm's length from his day-to-day duties. Nebraska's administration wanted a change in leadership at the top of the athletic department. The 2020 season was NU's fourth straight losing season, its worst stretch in modern program history.

On July 14 NU named Trev Alberts as its next athletic director after reportedly kicking the tires on several names, including Iowa State's Jamie Pollard and Huskers volleyball coach John Cook.

One thing was immediately noticeable when Alberts was announced as NU's next athletic director. Frost was nowhere to be seen in the room. He was on his way back from a family vacation in Colorado. Instead of holding the formal announcement one more day, they conducted the event without their head football coach in the room. His presence was not a priority.

Like Frost's hiring in 2017, this was another native son coming home. Alberts was a former NU All-American rush end in 1993. He also won the Butkus Award that year. His No. 34 was retired by Nebraska. Frost was Tom Osborne's starting quarterback on his final national championship team in 1997. However, Alberts' hiring was not meant to pair two former Huskers legends on the stage together.

If those few weeks of June and July were not the start of the writing on the wall, Frost's first meeting with Alberts on July 17, 2021, set the tone for their relationship. Frost and Alberts met in Omaha. It was a meeting Frost called with Alberts to discuss the future of NIL, which had just come into effect on July 1, 2021. The two met at an undisclosed location before an NIL event later at Happy Hollow Country Club in Omaha. A group of high-powered NU boosters were gathering to discuss the newly introduced name, image, and likeness plans at Nebraska. It was a meeting that laid the foundation of one of the first collectives in college athletics—several months before anyone realized this would eventually drive the NIL world we now live in.

Before that presentation led by Frost's close friend and former Nebraska attorney general Jon Bruning, Alberts met with Frost at a different location. Multiple sources have said it was a very tense encounter, one where Alberts marked his territory over his new head coach by noting that things needed to show signs of improvement and happen fast. At that point, Frost was on the clock.

* * *

Call it bad luck, poor roster management, bad coaching, or whatever you want. Scott Frost's time at Nebraska was unlike any era in the program's modern history. Nobody saw this coming. "Scott Frost is built for success, and I'm going to tell you: he will win multiple national titles at Nebraska. He will be competing for a Big Ten title within three years and he could be the next generation's Nick Saban," FOX's Tim Brando said on September 3, 2018, on *The Paul Finebaum Show*.

When Frost entered the room for his first Big Ten Media Days in July 2018, one Michigan writer whispered, "That's the next Urban Meyer of this conference." Media Days took place in Chicago. "We'll see how the first year goes," Frost told reporters. "But people better get us now because we're going to keep getting better and better."

A capacity crowd filled Memorial Stadium on September 1, 2018, to watch Frost coach his first game against Akron. Frost was fresh off a perfect 13–0 season at Central Florida, where he was named the national college football coach of the year. He was expected to immediately come to Lincoln, Nebraska, with a magic wand and return the program to glory.

However, things did not get off the ground in the 2018 season opener, as the game was canceled for lightning minutes after the opening kickoff. Instead of waiting around in Lincoln to play Sunday morning, Terry Bowden's Akron team got their check and left town. That set the stage for a 0–6 start in 2018. Frost's first win would not come until October 20 against Minnesota. His team finished 2018 with a 4–2 record down the stretch, including a game where they had Urban Meyer's No. 3 Ohio State team on the ropes. "I get it that that was a two-win team," Meyer said following his team's 36–31 win against Nebraska on November 3. "But that's a two-win team that people don't want to play right now...very good players, very good scheme, and guys that are going to get very good."

Nebraska's 4–2 finish in 2018 and comments like this by Meyer had the Huskers ranked in the preseason AP top 25 in 2019. They were also picked by many to win the West division.

NU started the year with a shaky 35–21 win against South Alabama. They were a 35 ½-point favorite heading into the game—the largest number on the opening weekend point spreads in college football. They pillow fought with the Jaguars for two quarters until Maurice Washington, who was suspended for the first half, came off the bench and carried them to victory.

The Huskers traveled to Colorado the next week, where more than 30,000 Nebraska fans took over Folsom Field. It was one of the greatest stadium takeovers we've seen by Big Red fans in years. The No. 25 ranked Huskers had a 17–0 lead at halftime. NU fans were prepared to take over the streets of Boulder like an invading army. Nebraska started the second half of that game with possession of the football. It received a delay of game penalty to begin the quarter, and from there the rest is history. The Buffaloes scored 34 points after halftime to win 34–31 in overtime. It was a moment that changed the trajectory of the Frost era, as more than 30,000 Huskers fans walked out of Folsom Field with their heads down, being taunted by Colorado fans with obscene gestures. Sophomore quarterback Adrian Martinez was a preseason Heisman dark horse in 2018. The loss at Colorado knocked him and the Huskers off their pedestal. "We let our fans down, we let Coach Frost down, and I wanted this game, and we wanted this game," Martinez said.

"I told those guys in the locker room, 'Remember this feeling. Let's not feel it again.'"

After the Colorado loss, however, they appeared to weather the storm, winning 44–8 against Northern Illinois the following week and 42–38 at Illinois. ESPN *College GameDay* came to Lincoln for the Ohio State game the following week. It was the show's first appearance in Nebraska since 2007, when the Huskers took on No. 1 ranked USC. NU's administration rolled out the announcement and plans for its new Go Big $165 million football facility project to capitalize on the stage *GameDay* was providing. None of it mattered. The Buckeyes raced out to a 48–0 lead in the third quarter. In a season where the Huskers got off to a 4–2 start, they finished 5–7, blowing leads of 17–0, 14–3, and 10–0 in losses to Colorado, Indiana, and Purdue.

That offseason Frost fired his offensive coordinator Troy Walters and special teams coordinator/outside linebackers coach Jovan Dewitt. This was the first time in Frost's young head coaching career that he had been forced to make staff changes.

* * *

It was early March of 2020. The world was days away from changing forever. Newly named Big Ten commissioner Kevin Warren was in Lincoln, Nebraska, as he tried to make his way around the conference and visit every campus. During that week news reports surfaced about the COVID-19 virus as it entered the United States. In a June 2020 interview in Scott Frost's office, he vividly remembered a conversation with Warren. "The new Big Ten commissioner was on our campus about a week before we got shut down, and we saw this coming," Frost said. "He was actually working out in our staff weight room over here in the Hawks, and I went in, and we had a really nice conversation. He was awesome, and I asked him then, 'If we get shut down, are we going to get our spring practices back even if it's later?' And he guaranteed me we would. Now, a lot has changed since then. I haven't heard a lot of talk about getting those practices back, but now that some schools are getting their kids back as early as June 1, I have heard a little bit of a pickup in those conversations. I'm kind of doubtful that that will happen because not everybody in the country will be back at the same time and ready to do those things."

College football programs nationwide attacked the COVID-19 pandemic differently based on local state politics and guidelines. Nebraska was unique because governor Pete Ricketts did his best to implement more flexible guidelines. They were some of the least rigid within the Big Ten footprint. Frost and Ricketts kept a regular dialogue.

Frost and his chief of staff Gerrod Lambrecht saw this as an opportunity to create an edge if they could get their players back to Lincoln months earlier than everyone else in the conference. In May of 2020, no college football programs were thinking about developing a workout plan—let alone moving players back to campus. But Frost believed they could provide a much safer environment for student-athletes in Lincoln due to the state's low COVID-19 numbers and the protocols they put in place.

By May 2, 2020, the Huskers had around 100 players in Lincoln. Lambrecht partnered with the University of Nebraska Medical Center in Omaha to get COVID-19 tests for the players as they arrived. The old South Memorial Stadium locker room was converted into a drive-through testing center for players. It was one of the first in the country when considering where COVID-19 testing was in early May of 2020. Nebraska's football team was the first sports team arguably in the world to go through COVID-19 testing protocols. Nobody at that time was thinking about group testing athletes—let alone able get their hands on the tests.

Lambrecht had a unique background as Frost's chief of staff. Before he joined Frost at Central Florida in 2016, he worked for years in private business in the medical industry. He understood how to deal with medical companies and get things done. Each player was forced to quarantine upon arrival in The Village apartment dorms on campus. They were divided up into four groups:

- Players that have been in Lincoln only
- Players that have been in Nebraska only
- Players that came from a COVID-19 hotspot
- Players that traveled out of Nebraska but not from a deemed hot spot

During the quarantine period at The Village apartment dorms, a day's worth of food was left outside their doorstep. Once they cleared quarantine, players were allowed to lift weights in voluntary groups of nine or fewer, which was compliant with state of Nebraska guidelines.

However, they faced a hurdle after the University of Nebraska closed its campus, making the normal NU weight room facilities off limits. Gym spaces in Lincoln, though, were open during COVID-19 as long as they adhered to state and local guidelines. Nebraska players had access to an off-campus warehouse they paid a monthly membership to use. Instruction was not allowed by NU coaches, but supervision was provided onsite. NU's compliance department was aware of this, and everything was within the rules if the workouts were deemed voluntary and held off campus with no instruction.

Everything was working out beautifully for Frost as he figured out a way to have his team train together when nobody else in college football was that far ahead in May of 2020. On July 13, 2020, the NCAA Division I Football Oversight Committee allowed teams to return to campus and conduct organized workouts with a regular season start date of September 5. On August 5, 2020, the Big Ten announced a 10-game conference-only schedule for its members, and the Huskers were slated to open at Rutgers on September 5 before hosting Illinois and Wisconsin in Lincoln for the next two weeks. It seemed advantageous on paper toward Nebraska's win total, as the states of New Jersey, Illinois, and Wisconsin were all heavily regulated with COVID-19 restrictions, and those teams had completed far less work together than Nebraska's roster had at that time.

Then, on August 11, 2020, Big Ten teams around the conference were called off from the practice field. The Big Ten officially canceled the 2020 season. Warren said the decision would not be revisited and was final. Reports of myocarditis and its link to COVID-19 were a driving factor to shut things down. Later, those reports would be debunked by several medical experts.

A day before the league's decision, Frost had an idea it was coming down the pipes and tried to get in front of it. He challenged the league. "Sometimes a head coach's responsibility is to fight for what the [players] want," Frost said. "Our football players want to play, the coaches want to coach, we want to play football this year at the University of Nebraska. Our players feel safe, they feel taken care of, and they want to play. I think what's kind of being missed in a lot of these conversations is what the world looks like, what universities look like, and what the lives of our kids look like if we don't play football. I haven't heard a lot of people talk about that. But what does the world look like without football? A lot of people around the country are going to point that all these decisions are going to be financial. Let's skip past that for a second. Let's skip past the fact the University of Nebraska will lose $80 to $120 million if we don't play football. The city of Lincoln will lose upwards of $300 million if we don't play football. Let's skip past the fact a lot of people are going to be laid off, furloughed, or lose jobs, and their kids aren't going to be able to have the same things that they have right now while their mom and dad are working. Let's skip past the fact a lot of schools are going to have to drop sports, and some sports may never exist again. Let's take the financial piece completely out of it.

"I want to stop and talk for a minute about what their lives look like if we cancel football tomorrow. If we cancel football tomorrow, we are throwing up the white flag and saying this can't be done. If that's the decision that's made, I'll certainly abide by it, but let's think about our players and their well-being for a minute. Do we keep them here or send them home? Where do they go, and what do they do? What do I do with them? The virus is going to be here if we play football or not, and our kids are going to have an opportunity to contract the virus if we are playing football or not. I still haven't seen a lot of evidence that kids are getting it in these activities. We feel, and I feel 100 percent certain, that the safest place for our players is right here, where there is structure, where there's testing, where there's medical supervision, where they have motivation to make smart decisions to stay away from the virus because if they don't, they are going to lose what they love and lose their opportunity to play football. The virus is here either way, and I would contend that our players are safer here doing what they love and being monitored and screened constantly than they would be if we sent them home. They have better access to medical care here. If we send them home, are they going to have doctors screening them for symptoms? Are they going to have people taking care of them? Are they going to have access to medical care if they do contract the virus? I truly believe at the bottom of my heart our players are safer with the testing and the things we can do for them here than if we cancel the season and send them somewhere else."

The national media heavily criticized Frost for those views. Reporters like *Sports Illustrated*'s Pat Forde took great pleasure in attacking Frost, even though Ohio State had similar views on playing football in 2020. The problem was that Nebraska was not Ohio State, and the national media felt Frost and the Huskers fans needed to know their place, where they stood. "Are the Cornhuskers slow learners, tone deaf, willfully belligerent, or still clinging to an outdated sense of blueblood entitlement?" Forde wrote.

ESPN's Desmond Howard even suggested the Big Ten should kick Nebraska out of the league for Frost's remarks. "I would demand a public apology from Nebraska," Howard said during an appearance on ESPN's *Get Up*. "And if I'm Kevin Warren, I'm working on a way to get their ass out of the Big Ten. They ain't Notre Dame, baby. They don't have that cachet. All the teams and coaches want to play, but they're not whining and crying."

The Big Ten eventually played in 2020. Another chapter to this saga was on August 27, 2020, when eight Nebraska players—Garrett Snodgrass, Garrett Nelson, Ethan Piper, Noa Pola-Gates, Alante Brown, Brant and Brig Banks, and Jackson Hannah—filed a lawsuit. Former Nebraska state senator and now U.S. congressman Mike Flood represented the eight players. Once the suit was filed, the Big Ten had just a few hours' notice to appear on a call with Lancaster County judge Susan Strong. An unprepared lawyer, Andrew Luger out of Minneapolis, represented the Big Ten and argued the case. The players demanded the league show voting proof of the Big Ten's Council of Chancellors and the president's initial decision to cancel the 2020 football season. The Big Ten had until August 31 to file a written brief in response to the motion. The eventual tally was released, and the presidents voted 11–3 not to play in 2020. The Big 12, SEC, and ACC conferences were all playing football in 2020, including Notre Dame, who joined the ACC that season as a temporary full-time member.

Nebraska's efforts eventually paid off. We got football in 2020, but the Huskers got a new schedule in return. Instead of opening at Rutgers, they played at Ohio State. Then they had games against Wisconsin, at Northwestern, and Penn State the next three weeks. Five of their eight games were on the road, including a December 18 Friday night season finale at Rutgers.

Only parents and media were allowed to attend Big Ten football games that season. Most other leagues in the country were capping attendance numbers around 25 percent capacity.

Everything about that 2020 season was ugly. It didn't start until October 24, which meant Nebraska's players had been on campus for six months lifting and training with no break. It was too much during a time in the country when everyone else was sitting at home and watching Netflix. NU was 2–5 heading into that finale at Rutgers, where parents were not allowed to attend due to New Jersey's COVID guidelines. They had bad losses to Minnesota and Illinois earlier that season, where the Huskers were more than double-digit favorites in both contests. The season would have had a completely different feel if they had won those two games. By the time December 18 came around, most of NU's players were done. Adrian Martinez was banged up. Wide receiver Wan'Dale Robinson had cracked ribs. Running back Dedrick Mills battled injury for most of the season. When the Huskers won 28–21 at Rutgers, nothing about that night felt right. They had four turnovers compared to one for Rutgers. They rushed for 365 yards and put up 620 yards of total offense yet barely won the game in an empty SHI Stadium. We saw the best and the worst of the Huskers in one night, which was a microcosm of the Frost era at times.

After the win, word got out that NU would qualify for a bowl game with a 3–5 record. There were no win requirements to play in a bowl game in 2020. Nebraska had not played in a bowl game since 2016. So it seemed like a no-brainer, and most thought they would take the invitation and extend the season. Bill Moos already had multiple bowl options lined up for the team.

However, immediately after the game, players like Martinez and Robinson put up doubt that the Huskers would accept a bowl invitation. Many NU players purchased plane tickets to fly home that weekend for the Christmas holiday. A bowl game more than likely meant Nebraska would play between the window of December 26 and December 30. That meant nobody was going home for Christmas after being on campus since early May without a break. The team got back from Rutgers around 3:00 AM that Saturday morning. Frost called at a team meeting around noon to have a player vote on the bowl game. This would be one of his most questionable leadership decisions as a head coach. His entire defense and defensive staff wanted to play in a bowl game. Several of his key players on offense did not, including the line. It was a tense Saturday in North Stadium. Multiple votes and discussions happened. The offensive line would not budge on their vote. Martinez would've been doubtful for the game, meaning true freshman Logan Smothers would've started. Quarterback Luke McCaffrey had already shut down for the season and took his shoulder pads off before kickoff at Rutgers. He would transfer from Nebraska a month later. Robinson also would have been out with his rib injury at Rutgers and transferred from the program in January of 2021. If a bowl game had happened in 2020, it would have been a different-looking team.

The irony of that moment was that Frost fought so hard to play football in 2020. When they had one more opportunity to play, his team did not show that same level of fight in return. They quit on Frost. Many things happened in the 2021 and 2022 seasons that solidified Frost's firing, but it's hard not to go back to 2020, which was the beginning of the end for Frost.

When Frost took the Nebraska job in December 2017, he had offers from Florida and Tennessee. He was the most sought-after head coach candidate in the country that year. He really contemplated taking the Nebraska job, knowing the pressure he faced to turn around his home state Huskers. The deciding factor for Frost was that he figured at Nebraska he would get extra time to turn things around compared to maybe Florida and Tennessee. Former head coach and athletic director Tom Osborne played a factor in convincing Frost to return home.

In the end, everything that could've gone wrong for Frost did. On top of finishing 16–31 in just more than four seasons, his father, Larry Frost, passed away in 2020. He also was in the process of raising a young family with three children under the age of five. Frost made it known immediately to the local media that he and his private life were off limits. This created an underground world of rumors and speculation about Frost, especially why his football team was not winning games. All of this ate at Frost and added to the mounting pressure he faced to turn his alma mater around.

Those close to Frost will tell you he was almost relieved it was over after Trev Alberts fired him three games into the

2022 football season. "Hopes were really high, maybe unrealistically high because when you take over a program with a losing record you're not going to automatically go undefeated and play for a national championship," Osborne said. "It takes a while, but still I think it was hard on everyone. For whatever reason a lot of the self-image that people have regarding Nebraska does revolve around Nebraska football. Certainly not everyone, but there's a fair number of people that put that as a very high priority. When that isn't going well, I think it affects to some degree the psyche of the state overall. You don't have a Nebraska State. You got one major school, where most states will have one, two, three, or four major universities in divided loyalties, but here you don't have that. As a result I think it leads to greater scrutiny. If you look at the newspapers, there are very few editions of the paper that don't have something about Nebraska football 365 days a year. Most other places once the season's over, there'll be a little bit about recruiting or something, but they're not going to have something every day in March, April, May, June, July, and then maybe by August things kind of ramp up a little bit. There isn't an offseason in terms of public scrutiny in the state, and in a way, it's a good thing, and in a way, it's extra burden for a coach."

Osborne understood the pressure Frost faced, but at the same time, he also supported the decision Alberts made. "Enduring that kind of scrutiny and criticism is difficult for anybody," Osborne said. "I feel very bad about what happened, but Scott was a good player here and had a great success. As an assistant at Oregon and then at UCF, he was probably the most sought-after coach in the country after his undefeated season at UCF. Anyway, it didn't work out, but there were some things that were somewhat beyond his control, and then other things that for whatever reason just didn't fall into place."

PART 2

THE LEGENDS

6

1960s Legend: Bob Brown

BOB BROWN WAS ONE OF THE FIRST PROGRAM LEGENDS IN Nebraska's long history of producing offensive linemen. The 6'4", 280-pound Brown's list of accomplishments is a long one. He was head coach Bob Devaney's first All-American in 1963. Brown was the first African American to receive All-American honors in school history and he became the first Huskers player to be inducted into both the NFL and College Football Hall of Fames. He accomplished the former feat in 2004.

A Cleveland native, Brown passed away on June 16, 2023, at 81. He is one of just three players in school history to have their jersey number (No. 64) permanently retired, joining Heisman Trophy winner wide receiver Johnny Rodgers (No. 20) and linebacker Tom Novak (No. 60). Nicknamed "Boomer," Brown became a first-round draft pick in the NFL and AFL in 1964. He played 10 seasons in the NFL for the Philadelphia Eagles, Los Angeles Rams, and Oakland Raiders. He's the only NFL player in history to be named All-Pro on three teams. Brown was named first-team All-Pro five times and second-team All-Pro four times. He played in six Pro Bowls and was named to the NFL's 1960 All-Decade team.

Brown was dominant in every metric. Very few Huskers did it at the level of Brown—both in the collegiate and NFL ranks. He's one of handful of guys from his time where you could make a case that his skillset would even translate to today's era. "He was a giant. I just remember he had such long arms in pass protection," former Nebraska and NFL offensive lineman Barney Cotton said of Brown. "He was just like a brick wall. He was the epitome of what they want linemen to be like now because he was tall, he was long, and he had great feet. Now, that same guy, he'd weigh a lot more obviously with strength training and stuff that they do now. His body type was such because he had such length and great feet that he'd be a Pro Bowler now."

Despite all of this, Brown lived a low-profile life. He rarely wanted the spotlight. One of the only times he came back to Nebraska was in 2004, when former athletic director Steve Pederson retired his No. 64 jersey after he was inducted into the NFL Hall of Fame earlier that year. "We are proud to declare November 26 as Bob Brown Day," Pederson said. "No other Nebraska football student-athlete has made such an impact at the collegiate and professional levels. As Bob Devaney's first All-American, he paved the way for future success of Nebraska student-athletes. As great as he was on the field, he was a student first, and we are honored to bring him home to this institution to share his football and life experiences with us."

* * *

When Bob Devaney took the Nebraska job in 1962, he knew that there was talent on the roster. I'm not sure he knew there was this much, though. Bill Jennings could recruit. He brought several future NFL players to Lincoln, Nebraska, that Devaney helped develop on his early teams. Bob Brown topped that list. "The thing that was interesting was that when Bob Devaney came here, they really had some good players," former assistant and eventual head coach Tom Osborne said. "They were 3–6–1 the year before Bob came. I think Bob and his staff came here, and they thought, *Hey, this is a little better than what we thought it was going to be.* Because you had Lloyd Voss who played in the NFL, you had Bobby Hohn who played in the NFL, you had Kent McCloughan, who played in the NFL, you had Bob Brown who played in the NFL, and John Kirby. They had some really good players. They went 9–2 that first season."

Many credited Devaney for getting the most out of Brown. Early in his career, Brown did not enjoy practice and often needed motivation from Devaney for his best to come out. This was Devaney's specialty. He was a master motivator. "Bob Brown needed a lot of encouragement to practice. He hated to practice," Mike Devaney, the son of Bob Devaney said. "I can remember he was always faking an injury or something so he didn't have to practice. I remember my dad would be sitting over there talking…Brown was standing there in his sweats and without a helmet on. My dad said to the two of [the staffers] standing there—he said it loud enough so Brown could hear him—'I'm not sure Brown is tough enough to play this game. Maybe I'll just have him clean out his locker.'

"Two seconds later Brown said, 'Hey, Bob, I hate the coach. I'm ready. I can go in.'

"He had a way of doing that. I can remember Carel Stith one time came off the field. Somebody had knocked him on his ass, and he grabbed a hold of him and he said, 'Caroline, are you going to hit him with your purse or are you going to knock him on his ass?'"

At the line of scrimmage, there was nobody better in his era, but his big body was not built to run long distances, Osborne remembers an example of that. It was October 26, 1962. The Huskers were getting ready to play Colorado in Boulder. "He'd always heard about the altitude. He lines up on one goal line and he goes. He sprints 100 yards," Osborne said. "This was on Friday, the day before the game. He crosses the goal line after 100 yards and flops, so the altitude got him. Bob Brown never ran 100 yards in Lincoln. That just shows you the mental aspect of the game now. It wasn't that he played badly out there. He was a great player, and I remember him quite well."

Devaney knew how to push Brown's buttons as well as anyone. "He hated working. He hated running," Mike Devaney said of Brown. "He had feet that must have been size 20. His feet hurt all the time. He hated to run. My dad always had to find some way of getting him going. I can remember one time in practice, he said, 'You know Bobby, see those guys sitting over in the stands? Those are pro scouts.'

"He said, 'Oh, really?'

"They got him running that way. I think he told him something similar in the football game, too. He said, 'You know, Bobby, really, if you stand out.' Bob liked to play in the games. He just didn't want to practice. When he realized what he could do—and I think probably the coaches there helped him a lot to realize that—and when they were successful and stuff, I think Brown fed off of that, too, and I think he realized himself what he could accomplish and what he could do."

However, when Brown wanted to run, there were very few better. Early in his career, he played on both the offensive line and as a linebacker. When Devaney took over from Jennings, he stopped playing two-platoon football and let players focus on just one side of the football. Brown stuck with the offensive line, even though he was probably an All-American-level defender. "My dad said for a man his size, he was the fastest man he ever knew," Mike Devaney said. "They used to run sprints 40 yards or whatever it was. The only guy that Brown couldn't beat—and he was the biggest man by far on the team—was Kent McCloughan, who was an Olympic-level sprinter. He was the only one that Brown couldn't beat in a 40-yard dash."

Brown's final piece of motivation at Nebraska came at the end of the 1963 season. The 9–1 Huskers took on 9–1 Auburn in the Orange Bowl on New Year's Day in 1964. The game marked one of the first times Auburn faced a team with African American players. The SEC did not have Black football players in 1963. The first in league history was not until 1967 at Kentucky. The Tigers would not have a Black player until 1969. Heading into the game in Miami, this got Brown's attention.

According to former media relations director Don Bryant, there was a concern going into the game. Devaney instructed Bryant to talk to Brown about the racial difficulties he might run into, but as you can imagine, there wasn't much that scared the massive lineman from Cleveland.

Bryant said that Devaney was only looking out for his star player, but Brown was not afraid going into the game. "Relax, Mr. Bryant, I've had a deep-seated animosity toward the great state of Alabama," Bryant recalled Brown telling him in his *Tales from the Nebraska Sidelines* book.

It didn't take long for Brown to show he wasn't scared. On the game's second play, Brown drove a Tigers defensive lineman 30 yards down the field, paving the way for Dennis Claridge's 68-yard touchdown run that put the Huskers up 7–0. NU won the game 13–7, giving the Huskers their first Orange Bowl victory in school history.

After his successful college career, Brown wasted no time transitioning to the NFL. Former Nebraska All-American linebacker Jerry Murtaugh did not play with Brown at NU, but the two program legends got to know each other later. Murtaugh had one of the few more recent interviews with Brown on his Saturday morning radio show in Omaha, Nebraska. He has a unique way of getting some Huskers from the past to open up more than normal. Brown shared a legendary story when he faced off against the Pittsburgh Steelers. "Bob Brown was the only man in the NFL that made All-Pro with three different teams. Did you know that?" Murtaugh said. "This man was something else. I had him on my show and I talked to him. I said, 'You've got to give me a good story.'

"He finally says, 'All right, I'm playing against Steelers and I'm going against big, bad Joe Greene. I was killing him. Finally, I come up to the line, and Greene screams at the other defensive tackle and said, 'Get your ass over here. I'm sick of this.'

"Bob said, 'I'm waiting for him to change positions.' The other guy comes over. I frickin' buried him, too. He said his helmet was off his head. I think he lost his shoes when I hit him. I'm standing there, and he gets up and he runs over to Greene and said, 'Fuck you, you get back to your own position.' Bob was laughing so hard. He said, 'I killed them both.'"

Brown's former coach George Allen of the Rams, a future Hall of Famer, had some powerful words to summarize his career: "At his best no one was better than big Bob Brown."

Hall of Famer Deacon Jones, a former teammate of Brown's, concurred with Allen. "He's a linebacker in an offensive lineman's body," Jones said about Brown. "He had a cold-blooded mentality. He'd kill a mosquito with an ax."

After playing for Philadelphia (1964–68) and Los Angeles (1969–70), Brown would finish his career playing in Oakland for the legendary John Madden (1971–73). Madden recalled how Brown marked his territory in Oakland immediately. He joined an offensive line with four future NFL Hall of Famers in Art Shell, Gene Upshaw, Jim Otto, and Ron Mix. "He hits a goal post with his forearm. *Crack!* And the whole goal post goes right down. All the guys are looking," Madden said in an NFL Films interview. "He turned around and walked off the field."

Maybe the biggest disappointment for Brown was how long it took him to receive his NFL Hall of Fame induction. He waited more 30 years to get into the Hall of Fame despite having a resume worthy of being a first-ballot member. "I was disappointed after the first five years out of ball. I thought I'd have been nominated and elected after that long. But it didn't happen," Brown told the *Lincoln Journal Star* in 2004. "After a decade or so, I finally let it go."

7

1970s Legend: Johnny Rodgers

THE ONLY THING THAT COULD EVER GET IN THE WAY OF Johnny Rodgers succeeding at Nebraska was himself. When the Omaha Tech High product came to NU, his Huskers career was nearly over before it started. On the last day of his freshman year in the spring of 1970, Rodgers and a group of friends devised a plan to rob a gas station in what they later called a "prank gone bad." They walked away from the gas station with $90, and that nearly cost him almost everything.

Initially, Rodgers was charged with armed robbery, but it was pleaded down to felony larceny, and he was sentenced to two years of probation. Before this happened Rodgers was regarded as one of the top freshmen the program had ever seen. Most incoming players at that time played freshman ball and then redshirted the next season before being elevated to the lower units in their third year. There wasn't even a thought of redshirting Rodgers after his freshman year in 1969. "I was the freshman coach when Johnny was in his first year there," former assistant coach Jim Walden said of Rodgers. "He was too good, man. There was no redshirt for him. By the end of his freshman year, he was No. 1 as a sophomore. He was just a great little athlete."

It was a much different time in college football, where freshmen everywhere had to earn their stripes. It wasn't until 1972 that the NCAA allowed freshmen to play at the varsity level.

"Probably the four years I was there, we might have had maybe half a dozen guys that were good enough to do that," Walden said. "He was a combination of punt returner, wide receiver, and a game-break athlete—best football player doing those things that I was ever around."

Walden said the 1970 incident with Rodgers changed him for the better. Rodgers knew he was very fortunate after what happened, and it raised his focus to a level that produced arguably the greatest player in program history. "He was pretty calm because he got himself into a little trouble dicking around with some guys about robbing a store or something, which stupid freshmen in college will do to try to prove they can do something. It never dawned on him that it was illegal," Walden recalled. "That was a little bit of a burden over him...It might have been one of the best things for him because it kept him in a low-profile mindset. After that thing came out and he got deferred, in my mind it made Johnny Rodgers be a little less cocky in a sense of what he might have been if he hadn't had that. In some ways it might have been a blessing personality-wise. That's the way I saw it. That's the way I believed it affected him. I don't think there was a question. He could have been a pretty cocky little dude if he'd wanted to be, but that kept him at bay with that thing hanging over his head."

* * *

All-American linebacker Jerry Murtaugh was well aware of Johnny Rodgers. Like Rodgers, Murtaugh was from North Omaha. He was the team tough guy who picked fights and stood up to any challenge. He also came from an era of football where sophomores were not given the keys to the offense. He quickly figured out in 1970 that Rodgers was not your typical sophomore. "He was a sophomore when I was a senior and he came in cocky and he did some bullshit on the field," Murtaugh said of Rodgers. "I threw him down one day. The coaches come over and screamed at me for throwing him down. I said, 'You tell that kid when that whistle blows—he stops.' He wouldn't do it. He kept jumping and shit. One day I just grabbed him, shook him, threw him down. I go, 'Jeez, coaches, he's a sophomore. I'm a senior.' They must have known something I didn't. That's how Johnny came in. He was really cocky. Yes, but he was a great football player. One thing I admired about him: he never had a fair catch. He said, 'Screw that. I want the ball.' I go, 'I can appreciate somebody like that.'"

Former wide receiver and assistant coach Guy Ingles was also very familiar with Rodgers. He played against him at Omaha Westside. They later played the same position at NU.

Ingles has been around many talented players during his football career, but he can't recall one that impacted the game more than Rodgers. "He is the best football player I've ever seen to this day," Ingles said. "The only one that's even comparable is Reggie Bush. Johnny was a triple threat. He could have been a defensive back, too. He was right where he should be though.

He was in the perfect offense with the perfect head coach, offensive coordinator, whatever you want to call it, and the rest is history. I've said that to a number of people, and they say, 'Well, what about Gale Sayers, or what about…' Sure there might be others, but if you want a guy that can beat you on a football field more ways than anybody I ever saw, it's Johnny Rodgers."

Former Huskers offensive lineman and assistant coach Barney Cotton didn't play with Rodgers, but he grew up watching him as a young boy in Omaha. "My dad was the athletic director at Omaha Burke. When I was growing up, there were times that I would go watch high school games. I saw Johnny play in high school first. Oh, my goodness," Cotton said. "There was probably seven or eight plays like that Oklahoma punt return he did in the Game of the Century. He was something. Johnny Rodgers was maybe the most exciting high school player I've ever seen. He was unbelievable."

During that Game of the Century against Oklahoma, Rodgers delivered a defining moment in Nebraska football's history with his 72-yard punt return in Norman, Oklahoma. That game set the stage for the Huskers' win and put Rodgers' name on the map to capture the 1972 Heisman Trophy.

Walden was in Norman that day for the Game of the Century. "I'm on the sidelines, and it was just so intense that you could not believe it," Jim Walden said. "Johnny Rodgers was the total difference. No matter what happened with Jeff Kinney and Jerry Tagge and Van Brownson and all those guys that played their hearts out, the guy that was the difference in the ballgame was Johnny Rodgers running the punt back. I'd never seen anything like it in my life. He grabs the punt in the middle of a boatload of Oklahomans, somehow or another did a spin to get out of the middle of it, spun back into the middle of it. Next thing I know, he is out and running down the sidelines and runs

72 yards for a touchdown. To me it depressed the Oklahoma people so badly…That just demoralized them. Because there had been so much talk about the Oklahoma running backs. They had a whole backfield full of great guys, and it was always Jerry Tagge, Van Brownson versus Johnny Rodgers and Jeff Kinney versus blah, blah, blah but always Rodgers. That punt return verified what every Oklahoman was afraid to death of: Johnny Rodgers. To me it just made everything go after that."

The punt return was vintage Rodgers, who did not believe in the fair catch. On a play that defined Nebraska football, placed Bob Devaney on the trajectory to his first national championship, and led to the school's first Heisman winner, many people held their breath on the Cornhuskers sideline. "He stood right in the middle of a swarm of guys and caught the punt," Walden said. "Everybody was like, 'Oh God, don't catch it'—*boom*—he catches it, takes a step, does a spin, jumps out. I don't know what he was doing, but all I know is, man, he was moving things and jumping sideways, and then all of a sudden, he's out of the spot of all those people, then down the sidelines. Of course, the Oklahoma people say everybody was clipping everybody, and that's the truth. But they didn't call it, so what the hell? Anyway, I would've said the same thing. It was bodies flying every which way—ours and theirs, trying to figure out where he was going. It was a 10, 12-second moment of unbelievable football ability. That, to me, centralized who Johnny Rodgers was. He was a big-time player and going to make a big-time play. There wasn't any bigger stage than that he'll ever be on."

To measure Rodgers' impact on Nebraska football, all you have to do is look in the school record book. Rodgers played in an era where teams only played 11 regular-season games, true freshmen didn't play on the varsity, and bowl game stats didn't count in the record book, but his name is still tied to several school records. Rodgers is the only non-quarterback to pass, rush, and catch a touchdown in the same game. His eight career kick/punt return touchdowns remain a school record. "Johnny Rodgers was exceptional, and things were built around him," Walden said. "The offensive staff, Tom [Osborne] in particular, did a good job of getting him in position to be the guy that helps us win games."

Rodgers is tied with several players for the school record with three receiving touchdowns in a game. His 25 career receiving touchdowns is still a school record and may never be broken. Rodgers had four 100-plus yard receiving games in 1971 and 1972, which were school records until 2017. He had 10 games of 100-plus receiving yards in his career. His 942 regular-season receiving yards was a school record until 2017. He held the regular-season record for receptions with 55 until 2007. He held the regular-season receiving touchdown record with 11 until 2013. Rodgers finished with 2,479 yards receiving, a school record until Kenny Bell broke it in 2014.

Rodgers caught a pass in all 37 games he played as a Huskers player from 1970 to 1972. That was a record until Stanley Morgan Jr. broke it in 2018, going 38 straight games with a reception. His 15.02 yards per all-purpose touch is also a record for an NU player with 100 or more touches in a season. Rodgers had 132 touches for 1,983 yards in 1971. "Johnny Rogers was 35 years ahead of his time as a kick returner and a receiver," Huskers historian Jim Rose said. "You watch the guy and his lateral movement, his quickness, his stop-start—you just don't see that. You don't even see that today. Rodgers was truly a game changer."

In a 1971 game against Oklahoma State, Rodgers had seven punt returns for 170 yards, which is still a school record. He held the school record for longest punt return at 92 yards until

Bobby Newcombe broke it in 2000. Rodgers still holds the NU bowl game record for longest punt return for a touchdown, going 77 yards against Alabama in the 1972 Orange Bowl. Not counting bowl games, Rodgers finished his career with a school-record 98 punt returns for 1,515 yards and seven touchdowns. He is also one of just two Huskers to ever return a punt and a kickoff for a touchdown in the same season.

Osborne is often regarded as one of the best offensive minds in college football history. Having a player like Rodgers to build upon during some of his early years as a playcaller helped Osborne's career take off. In Rodgers' final game as a Husker, Osborne moved him to running back for the 1973 Orange Bowl against Notre Dame. It was a move nobody knew was coming and one that solidified he was the most dominant player in college football. Rodgers ran for four touchdowns and passed for another in that game, helping the Huskers route Notre Dame 40–6. They became the first team ever to win three consecutive Orange Bowls.

When you count bowl games, Rodgers finished his Huskers career that night in Miami with 50 career touchdowns. "Johnny could probably hurt you more ways than anybody I ever coached," Osborne said. "He was a great receiver and he was a very good runner/ball carrier. I think his last game we played him at I-back, and he would've been a good I-back. He always wanted to play corner and he would've been a great corner. We just didn't want to wear him out because he was about 170 pounds and he was a punt returner and a kickoff returner. We had him carry the ball on some counter plays as well. As a receiver he probably could do his most damage. I always thought Johnny was worth 10 to 14 points a game just by having him. The thing that was really telling was the amount of field position he got you on returns. People sometimes don't understand how big a 20-yard return is versus a five-yard return and what it can mean. That extra 15, 20 yards that he was getting on his returns was substantial and added up to points."

When Rodgers won the 1972 Heisman Trophy, Osborne was with him at the ceremony. A few months later, he would officially take over the program from Bob Devaney. At that same Heisman Trophy ceremony, Huskers defensive lineman Rich Glover finished third. In 1970 and 1971, Nebraska captured its first two national championships in school history, but you can argue Rodgers winning the Heisman Trophy in 1972 was equally as big of a moment for the program.

Rodgers remains a well-known name to this day in college football despite playing more than 50 years ago. He's made as many Heisman Trophy public appearances as anyone that's ever won the award. "He still carries that trophy around," Osborne said of the Heisman's impact on him and his life.

8

1980s Legend: Mike Rozier

THE MOST DECORATED RUNNING BACK IN SCHOOL HISTORY is Mike Rozier. His path from New Jersey to Nebraska was a unique one. In 1980 it was known that Rozier would be a few credits short of academically qualifying. Several people were recruiting him before that, but most schools fell off once they realized Rozier was a non-qualifier.

Nebraska head coach Tom Osborne and assistant coach Frank Solich decided to stick with Rozier. They developed a plan that would get him to Lincoln, Nebraska. He attended Coffeyville Community College in 1980, leading them to a 9–0 record and rushing for 1,157 yards and 10 touchdowns on 157 carries. Osborne had a relationship with Coffeyville's legendary head coach Dick Foster, which got Rozier closer to

Lincoln and made his transition in the spring of 1981 much easier. This plan would eventually deliver Osborne's only Heisman Trophy winner as a head coach and the school's only 2,000-yard rusher in history. There have been just two other Heisman winners who have attended a junior college—USC running back O.J. Simpson (City College of San Francisco) and Auburn quarterback Cam Newton (Blinn College in Texas). "Everyone forgot all about me but Nebraska," Rozier said in a 1983 Independent Press Service article. "Tom Osborne suggested that I go to junior college to get my marks up. And he kept in touch with me to see how I was doing."

Rozier attended Coffeyville Community College in Kansas for the 1980 season. It was a huge change from Camden. He rode a Greyhound bus cross country and was dropped off in Coffeyville, which seemed like the middle of nowhere. "Everything was in one building," Rozier said. "There wasn't anything out there. It was hot. The bushes had all dried up. The grass had all dried up. There was no green grass."

Rozier was so miserable in Coffeyville he nearly quit football all together, but he decided to stick it out. He would go on to lead Coffeyville that perfect record. All of a sudden, Rozier was back on the map, and all of those people, who forgot about him a year ago, reappeared into his life after his All-American freshman season at Coffeyville. However, Rozier never forgot that Osborne was the only coach that stuck with him after word got out he wouldn't be eligible. Osborne's loyalty toward Rozier made it an easy decision for him to attend Nebraska. "Nebraska stuck with me," Rozier said. "So I stuck with Nebraska."

This became one of Nebraska's strengths over the years. Osborne was willing to wait on talented players to get their academics in line, knowing what resources they had at NU. Solich was the lead recruiter on Rozier. By 1980 the Huskers were also on the cusp of having one of their best runs in history under Osborne. By 1981 they would begin a run where they were in national championship contention each season, winning the Big 8 title four years in a row. "It wasn't hard to like Mike. He has a great personality," Solich said of Rozier. "I actually enjoyed going back to Camden and talking to him and I got involved with some teachers and the people that knew Mike a little bit because it became pretty clear that he was probably going to have to go to a junior college. I decided I didn't care. I was going to stick with him. Through all that time, we kept a relationship."

Solich was also beginning to develop quite a recruiting reputation in New Jersey. Not only did he bring Rozier from the Garden State, but he also landed All-American wide receiver Irving Fryar. Like Rozier, Fryar came to NU somewhat under the radar but would leave as one of its best receivers in history and he became the eventual No. 1 pick in the 1984 NFL Draft.

Nobody could've predicted Rozier would be a Heisman winner or that Fryar would be a future No. 1 draft pick. Solich saw something in both, and it played a big piece in history for Nebraska as Osborne built his 1980s Scoring Explosion offense, which also featured quarterback Turner Gill and had an offensive line that produced three consecutive Outland Trophy winners in Dave Rimington (1981–82) and Dean Steinkuhler (1983). "Frank Solich was a really good recruiter," Osborne said. "He got Mike Rozier and Irving Fryar, and Irving was the No. 1 pick in the NFL draft. [Fryar] was playing tight end or something, and they never threw him the ball. I remember watching the film, and Frank said, 'This guy is supposed to be a great athlete. I couldn't see it because of the offense they ran. They never threw him the ball. He never touched the ball.' Frank stayed with him. Irving came and then, of course, Mike.

"Frank was a good recruiter, and that was difficult because Frank had never been to New Jersey, and New Jersey is a different world. He flew in there and had to rent a car and had to find schools. At that time a lot of the coaches in New Jersey called the shots. They'd say to the player, 'You're going here; you're going there.' It wasn't so much the player's decision, but Frank was good with high school coaches and families. I always appreciated his ability to go back there and get players to come to Nebraska."

Nebraska became a well-respected program in the state. The high school coaches trusted Solich and Osborne. Landing players like Rozier and Fryar from New Jersey would pave the way for the future. "I knew they were talented," Solich said. "I don't know that they had the kind of reputation that maybe top recruits have now. They certainly deserved to be in the top echelon."

Other top New Jersey prospects like defensive linemen Jason and Christian Peter and linebacker Doug Colman eventually came to NU. Jason Peter said Solich was a big reason why.

"He was just a relationships guy," Peter said. "Any coach at least in the Shore Conference area—where I was and even as they got to meet other high school coaches over the years from North Jersey or South Jersey—they would all say the same thing: how much they loved when Frank would come in. That's what recruiting is. It's relationships. You know that. It's putting in the time. Even when that school doesn't have a kid, it's still stopping in, saying hello to the coaches. 'What kind of players do you have coming up?' Not just, 'What can you do for me right now?' Frank was a master at that. Obviously, he was good with parents. Parents always felt comfortable sending their child out to the school if coaches like Frank Solich were on staff. It was not a big deal for Christian and I. It wasn't a big deal for us to come out here. Our parents were more than comfortable with it. Frank, he was honest. Obviously, that all stems from the man at the top, and that trickles down. There's a certain way that you run the program, or you don't. The way that we ran under Coach Osborne was that there was honesty involved."

* * *

When Mike Rozier got to Nebraska in the spring of 1981, it did not take long to see his big-picture potential. However, the way Tom Osborne ran his program, it was extremely difficult for a newcomer to win a job immediately. The depth of Osborne's rosters was incredible. In 1981 NU also had running back Roger Craig, who would put up 13,100 total yards of offense and score 73 touchdowns during his decorated, 11-year career in the NFL.

Osborne ran a system where he platooned several players in games, resting his starters. It didn't take long for people to realize Rozier would be special. In fact, Mike Corgan's reaction was telling. "I remember the first scrimmage with Mike Rozier here, going down the sideline and making a guy miss and then going into contact and breaking it and scoring," Frank Solich said. "Coach Corgan would sometimes take his pipe out at practice, and I could see him. He adjusts his pipe and he adjusts his hat and he has a certain look in his face that he knew what he had there."

It was Rozier's running style that made him unique. He loved making first contact. He wasn't necessarily the fastest back, but his physical traits and ability to get up field were different. "A lot of times, people with a football under their arm can make you miss, but they're going to take a little time making you miss," Osborne said. "I mean, it'd be a couple of juke steps there before making you miss. Mike had the ability to be going up field, and hardly anything ever slowed him down. He'd leave people grasping air. He had an uncanny ability to be elusive. He probably didn't have sprinter speed. He was fast and he had reasonably good size. He was fairly strong. He could get yards after contact. He was a very complete back. Also, we had a good offensive line, which didn't hurt. We had a quarterback in Turner Gill, who also added a dimension that wasn't all on Mike to run the ball. We had a pretty good ability to spread the ball around. It wasn't just a one-man show, but Mike was very talented."

In 1981 Rozier split reps with Craig nearly 50/50. Both backs finished with more than 1,000 yards. It wasn't until 1982 when Rozier took over the top spot outright, while Craig split time at running back and even tried some fullback during his senior season. Rozier would rush for 1,807 yards and 15 touchdowns as a junior, setting up his nearly 2,300-yard Heisman season in 1983. "It didn't make a difference whether it was Oklahoma or Iowa State or Colorado or what have you. Those that were going to start that game, they'd probably go the first two or three series. Then the second team would rotate in," fullback Mark Moravec said. "Again, depending on how each player was performing, they may get in some additional reps—or again if they fumbled or jumped offside or went the wrong way, a broken play, which seldom happened—Corgan and [Osborne], they would just see the flow of the game and see who was being more effective against that, the opponent, and those were the guys who got a few more carries. There was times where Roger Craig was the leading rusher, and there was times when Mike was, but we also had guys like Brad Johnson, who backed up Rimington at center, who could have probably started at any school in the Big 8 at that time. We just would dominate them. Come third quarter, when the second and third team went in for good and the stars would sit, it would be demoralizing to the other team because they were just as damn near as good as our starters."

Rozier also ran with the toughness both Solich and Corgan preached. "The one thing you could see clearly about Mike was he could read blocks really well. As a fullback and even the linemen would tell you that," Movavec said, "Mike had a natural way of helping set up the blocker—whether it be a dip of a shoulder in and then he bounced out and just made it much easier for you as a blocker to put a block on that guy. He did that really, really well. He had a great sense of gravity. I mean, he ran low to the ground. I remember he always told me, 'Remember, we got to hit them before they hit us.' When someone was going to try and tackle him, he would try and hit them before they hit him. That was just his mentality.

"Obviously, one of the things that Corgan taught us: we had a drill where we had to drop our shoulder, and he said that, 'If you run to the right, the ball had to be in the right hand. If you're running to the left, ball had to be in the left hand. If someone's coming to put a tackle on you, if you are running to the right, the ball is in your right hand, you drop that left shoulder and lift it with your forearm to try and run through that tackle. Run through it.' Rozier had that perfected and all right away. It was something naturally that he could do. His sense of gravity, and he wasn't an overly fast guy, but he had that speed that he'd just get away from a guy and make it tough for guys to put a good lick on. Nobody ever hit him really hard and knocked him on his rear end. If he knew he was going to take a hit, his mentality was to hit them before they hit you."

Rozier certainly perfected that mentality in 1983. There may never be another year in Nebraska football history like that season that Rozier had. Rozier finished his career with a school record 4,780 rushing yards and 52 touchdowns. During his 1983 senior season, he set the school record by rushing for 2,148 yards and 29 touchdowns to become the Huskers' second Heisman Trophy winner—joining wide receiver Johnny Rodgers, who won the 1972 Heisman. To this day, only one other player has ever rushed for more than 4,000 yards in his career at NU (Ameer Abdullah). Rozier still remains the only NU running back to rush for more than 2,000 yards in a single season. What is remarkable about many of Rozier's numbers was that in several games he was pulled out early in the second half because the Huskers had such big leads. Rozier finished his career with a 7.16-yard-per-carry average on 668 attempts. That was an NCAA record until 2005 when USC running back Reggie Bush finished his career with a 7.3-yard per carry average.

Rozier was officially inducted into the College Football Hall of Fame in 2006. "Rozier's greatest strength was he just wouldn't go down," former play-by-play announcer and Huskers historian Jim Rose said. "He wasn't a gifted athlete. He was just tougher than shit. He just would not go down. That offense was a series of remarkable parts from Turner to Irving to Rozier to Craig to Jamie Williams, Rimington, and Dean Steinkuhler. Those two years, '82 and '83, it's pretty astounding the level of talent on that offense. Look at all the first-rounders. Steinkuhler was the second overall pick in the draft. Rozier was the first pick in the USFL draft. Fryar was the first pick in the [NFL] draft. Rimington went in the first round. Rimington was late first round only because they were worried about his knees. It was unbelievable material back in those days."

A two-yard touchdown run against UCLA highlighted Rozier's 1983 Heisman Trophy season. Yes, that's right. *Two yards.* The call was *49 Pitch* to the left side. It was completely bottled up, so Rozier crossed the field to his left, running between 80 to 90 yards to score from two yards out and change the game's complexion. NU went on to win 42–10. After two early fumbles, the Huskers started the game down 10–0 to the Bruins. Rozier's score put Nebraska up 14–10 before halftime, and the Big Red never looked back. "It seems like all of our Heisman Trophy winners have had one distinctive play that stood out," Moravec said. "He started off the pitch play to the left and reversed field and went back around the right and scored a touchdown. That got run on ESPN several times before other games and things like that. That was a play that was his signature statement, I think.

"I don't know that they lifted many weights or anything like that down in Coffeyville. He actually got bigger and stronger at Nebraska. He was a load to bring down. Even though I wasn't there in 1983, I just knew that he was going to continue to improve, and again one way to prevent yourself from getting hurt is by hitting the other guy before they hit you. That was just a simple thing that'll stick with me for the rest of my life."

To this day, Rozier remains a fixture at the Heisman ceremony in New York. Each year he is seen on stage at the Downtown Athletic Club dressed to the nines from head to toe. Former Huskers player Jimmy Burrow never played with or coached Rozier at Nebraska. However, the two did share a great Heisman moment in 2019 when Jimmy's son, Joe, won the award at LSU.

Burrow was coaching for Solich at Ohio, as he was his longtime defensive coordinator in Athens, Ohio. Once Rozier knew his connection to Solich, he demanded Burrow get him on the phone.

That's the type of impact Solich made on Rozier. He helped change his life, and to this day, he has a great relationship with his former position coach. "We were up pretty late one night, and Coach Solich was living in Athens. We were in the hospitality room at the Heisman, and he said, 'Let's call Frankie,'" Jimmy Burrow said. "I looked down at my watch and I said, 'Mike, it's like 2:00 in the morning there.'

"He said, 'Oh, he always answers my phone call.'

"I said, 'All right.' Mike called him, and sure enough, he answered, and we had a fun conversation for about 10 minutes. That was cool."

9

1990s Legend: Tommie Frazier

THE 1990S WERE A DEFINING DECADE FOR NEBRASKA FOOTBALL, as the program won three national championships and compiled a 60–3 record from 1993 to 1997. Perhaps no player defines the decade of the 1990s more than quarterback Tommie Frazier. The Florida native was the only four-year starting quarterback in history under Tom Osborne as he took over the job midway through his freshman season. In that era it was unheard of for a true freshman to play for Osborne—let alone start at a position like quarterback. Frazier was different in every which way.

From the minute Frazier walked on campus, Osborne knew he was different. He was a program-changing recruit for Osborne in 1992 just like quarterback Turner Gill was in 1980.

"Looking at his high school film, he was the best option quarterback I'd ever seen," Osborne said of Frazier. "I guess people call it dual-purpose, but he's very talented, and Kevin Steele was on our staff at that time and Kevin did a great job of recruiting Tommie. I went down and visited with him, and there were a lot of schools interested in him, but it came down to Nebraska. The first four or five games, he didn't start, but then we felt he was ready to go in there and start. He had a pretty good year. The last six, seven games, he played pretty well. We thought he had a great future. He was a great runner, a good decision-maker, took pretty good care of the ball, and was not necessarily a pure passer, but he was good enough to get the job done. He was very, very talented."

Frazier would leave NU with a 33–3 record as a starter, including an 11–2 mark against ranked opponents. He was 2–1 in national championship games and named the MVP in all three of them. Getting Frazier to pick Nebraska was no easy task. He was regarded by some as one of the best high school football players in the country and he provided a much-needed antidote for the Huskers.

Osborne's program had hit a wall after the 1991 season, losing to Miami 22–0 in the Orange Bowl and to Washington 36–21 in September of that year. The Hurricanes and Huskies split the national title in 1991. In 1990 NU lost to Georgia Tech in the Citrus Bowl and to Colorado during the regular season; those two teams split the national title that season. The Huskers were seemingly close, but the gap still felt sizeable. Osborne needed to do something different. They began switching their defensive scheme by 1992 to the more attacking 4-3. Before that the Huskers ran a 5-2 defense that relied on its coverage to play more of a soft shell on the back end. When they played teams with elite quarterback and wide receiver talent, they were no match on defense.

It was clear they also needed a spark at the quarterback position. Osborne and his staff zoned in on Frazier at Manatee High School in Bradenton, Florida. During that time Osborne turned his Florida recruiting over to Steele, a hotshot young assistant coach. He was instrumental in leading the charge to get Frazier interested in Nebraska.

The key selling point was the Huskers' offense. Teams like Miami, Florida, and Florida State were not interested in running the option. So Frazier was not interested in them. Of the top teams in the country, only Nebraska, Notre Dame, Clemson, and Colorado were running the option. "As talented as Tommie was, and you think about kids from Florida—that distance away, people that live in the south, and having the kids from there travel all the way here to go to school—that all seems like somewhat of a long shot, but obviously, Miami, Florida, and Florida State were looking for a different type of quarterback than Tommie," former assistant coach Ron Brown said. "I don't know how heavily he was recruited there. I don't know that it was a very heavy recruiting process, particularly for the quarterback position. I don't know, but he was certainly a good enough athlete to play there. The kind of style of quarterback that he was, I think Kevin knew that we would have a good chance because it came down to us, Notre Dame, and Clemson. I think Colorado got involved a little bit, but all four of those teams and us—all four of us were running the option. I can't think of anybody better in the country than Tommie Frazier in terms of running the offense. I think a lot of times in recruiting, making wise decisions on things like that are very important.

"Then Kevin was a very personable recruiter. He did a great job, I think, with the family, mom, and Tommie himself, so we got in the ballpark with it. Then I think the other thing I remember was that when Tommie visited in December, I'm sure he heard how cold it was up here in December, and we all know that it is, but for some reason on this particular day when Tommie came in for his recruiting trip, it was a 60 to 65-degree day. Every now and then we'd get a freak day, and that was one of them. That weekend was pretty wild. I remember just the word around when Tommie was on campus was that he had heard so much about how cold it was. He was actually saying, 'Ah, it's not that bad. I thought there was going to be pretty tough weather.' A lot of times when a kid goes and visits a place that's far away, he goes by what he sees right now. Oftentimes, he may not ask, 'Is this normal? Is this always the way it is?' I don't know what kind of answers he'd gotten had he asked that question, but I know it turned out good for us."

Huskers historian, former play-by-play announcer, and sideline reporter Jim Rose emphasized how crucial Steele was in landing Frazier. Steele earned the Frazier family's trust, ultimately leading to him picking Nebraska over Clemson. "He was very highly recruited. He was the *USA TODAY* National Player of the Year, but he wanted to play quarterback, and only four premier schools were running the option," Rose said. "Nebraska, Colorado, Notre Dame, and Clemson. He made it clear: 'I'm a quarterback. If your offense is not for me, then don't even bother to call.' Nebraska was in on that deal, but my understanding is he was convinced that he wanted to go to Clemson. After the visit to Clemson, he wanted to go to Clemson.

"His mom had gotten really close to Kevin Steele, and his mom said, 'You promised those coaches from Nebraska that you would make a visit. You can go to Clemson, but Nebraska needs to get a visit from you.' And he did. He just had a great time on the visit, and it was awesome. Man, he was a natural.

He was a pure option quarterback. I do remember watching him in practice because we had Mickey Joseph on the team and we had Tony Veland on the team playing quarterback and we had Mike Grant on the team playing quarterback. Brook Berringer, too. [Frazier] was a different athlete. He was just a totally different guy on the football field. It was pretty clear he was going to be the guy, and they didn't redshirt him and they redshirted almost every other freshman, but they didn't redshirt him."

In 1992 Osborne started Grant, who had been waiting in the wings behind Keithen McCant and Mickey Joseph in 1991. After a 29–14 loss at No. 2 Washington, it became clear Grant was not the answer. "We had lost to them the year before at home in a fairly close game to Washington," Brown said. "They had a series where we were backed up on our own 1-yard line, and Mike Grant was our quarterback. Mike was a soft-spoken kind of guy, and back then we weren't in shotguns and clapping, or the guard wasn't telling the center when to snap the ball. It wasn't that kind of day and age then. It was: get under center and bark out signals. You have the entire student body of Washington just ripping in a very loud stadium anyhow. We popped off about two or three penalties in a row half the distance to the goal line. I think we had the ball probably on the four-inch line trying to get out of there, and we couldn't get out of there. I know in my mind, too, Mike was a good player, good athlete, but Tommie clearly had a commanding presence about him. Tommie's command, when he came into a game—not only his talent, his ability to run the option, and all of that—but the command that he had in the game, the loudness of his voice, what he was in the huddle, what he was when he played, who he was after a play, just the command and the leadership taking over at that quarterback position."

Osborne was also under some pressure at this time, as his program had lost five bowl games in a row heading into the 1992 season. Colorado also recently had Nebraska's number in the Big 8 Conference. Frazier had been seeing top unit reps from the minute he stepped on campus. That was extremely rare for a quarterback under Osborne. But before he could make the move to start Frazier, he needed to know he was ready.

The day was October 24, 1992, at Missouri. Frazier made his first career start as a Husker. He was the first ever true freshman to start a game at quarterback for Nebraska and just the second ever true freshman quarterback to play in a game at NU, joining eventual All-American Steve Taylor, who saw action as a backup in 1985.

The move paid off. The team went 5–2 with Frazier at quarterback down the stretch, losing to Iowa State and then Florida State in the Orange Bowl. The loss in Ames in 1992 was completely out of character for Osborne's teams. It was the only time they lost a game as a favorite in his 25-year coaching career. In some ways that moment was needed to get Frazier ready for the years to come. "I always told [Osborne] I ruined his career," former Cyclones head coach and Bob Devaney assistant Jim Walden joked after his team's 19–10 win against Nebraska in 1992. "I ruined his record. We were the only bad team he ever lost to."

* * *

After nearly leading Nebraska to a national championship in 1993, Tommie Frazier was well on his way to becoming the top quarterback in college football in 1994. Frazier was rolling after impressive wins against West Virginia, Texas Tech, UCLA, and Pacific to start the 1994 season. Then, something felt different. "We noticed something. I know I did and I think a couple of other people noticed something maybe that Thursday before that Pacific game where it just didn't look like he was the same," Ron Brown said. "It looked like he was struggling a little bit for some reason. You could tell. You just thought maybe it's what you get normally in the middle of the season. Everybody's doing that. Then when he went down during that Pacific game...it was a shock."

Frazier was ruled out indefinitely with a blood clot. At the time some thought it could be a career-ending ailment. Frazier's blood clot became national news. Lincoln, Nebraska, doctors held a press conference to discuss it. The media filmed Frazier as he left Bryan Hospital in Lincoln. Suddenly, Osborne's national championship season looked in doubt. "Part of it was we were No. 1 or No. 2 in the nation," Brown said. "We're talking about arguably the best player in the country...A lot of it was the high-profile situation that we were in as a team."

Frazier was eventually cleared to play in the Orange Bowl against Miami. In his place, Brook Berringer went 7–0 as a starter, while Matt Turman won a game at Kansas State. The Huskers faced a familiar foe in Miami at the Orange Bowl. Tom Osborne faced a tough decision, as Berringer won over the locker room with his 7–0 showing as a starter, which included an impressive win against Colorado, who also was a national championship contender. It was arguably CU's best team of all time.

Like everything Osborne did, he had a process with how he would evaluate the two quarterbacks over the month of December. It was one of the most difficult decisions Osborne faced as a head coach. "The blood clots were a pretty serious deal because the doctors told us that he almost certainly wouldn't play the rest of the season, and he may never play again because the blood clot went the full length at the back of his leg, and they weren't sure if they'd be able to dissolve it or not. So they injected him with blood thinners and anti-coagulants," Osborne said of Frazier. "Then came the end of the season. We're getting ready for the bowl game, and he thought he'd be able to play, and they did clear him to play. We decided we'd play them both. Tommie started the game in the first quarter and had an interception or something. We were going to play Brook anyway, so we put Brook in the second quarter, and Brook did pretty well for a while, and then he had an interception, and so we put Tommie back in at the end. Tommie finished it up, and that's when we came from behind to win."

It was one of the most difficult personnel decisions Osborne ever managed in his coaching career, and he handled it perfectly. "One thing I liked about Coach Osborne, I've always loved this about him, and he's a human like we all are, and everybody has a hunch or favorites or different things particularly when it comes down to those difficult decisions, the intangibles, how you measure all that, how you do it. Tom still had his objectivity," Brown said. "He still graded every play, put it out there for those players. You know what? The decision was his at the end of the day, but he put it in the hands of the players. I think that's what good coaches do; they make tough decisions...The starter just isn't necessarily the finisher. I think, even though the starter in that game against Miami became the finisher, it took two of those quarterbacks to win it. They both were instrumental in us winning that game against Miami as well as that whole football season.

"Before Tommie went down, he had a great contribution to our team obviously. The West Virginia Kickoff Classic was huge playing back east and so forth. The way we started that season off to play, go on the road, and play a tough Texas Tech team down there, Tommie had a great day down there, and then we had a tough UCLA team here. For those few games, Pacific wasn't much of a match, but those first three games were challenges, and Tommie Frazier rose to the occasion. Then you had Brook Berringer come in and was fantastic through the heart of that season, and it allowed him to flourish. Then, of course, when you come down to the end of the season there and you have to make a tough decision, you have to have some level of objectivity that Tom put in the hands of those players and some level of gut during the game as to when to take the one out, put the other one in. Somehow, some way, Coach Osborne got that done, but I think he does it foundationally. I don't think it's all subjective. I think there is some objectivity, but I think he does have a feel as well as, *hey, maybe this is the series that I ought to get Tommie back in the game*, or *this is the series that Brook ought to come in*, and he throws that touchdown pass. You look back at it all, and it all to me makes sense."

One of Nebraska's greatest players in program history never won a Heisman Trophy and was never voted a captain by his teammates. The captain snub in 1995 was very interesting, considering Frazier was regarded as such a great on-field leader. It spoke more about the personality of Frazier. Sometimes being named captain is more of a popularity contest. Frazier was not necessarily popular with the locker room. He's never been shy with his words even to this day. "He had high expectations and, of course, he played down there at Manatee High School," Osborne said. "He was pretty used to winning and he had pretty high standards for himself and other people. He was not afraid to call people out. If somebody missed a block or somebody wasn't performing up to speed, he would sometimes call attention to it in the huddle or whatever. It doesn't necessarily win a popularity contest, but on the other hand probably to some degree, it keeps people on their toes, so he is a very good competitor. It's odd that he wasn't elected captain because of his prowess and the position of being a quarterback, but I think some of that played into it a little bit. He was still a very strong leader on the football team."

Defensive lineman Jason Peter said Frazier not being named a captain wasn't a snub but more a reflection of the overall leadership the 1995 Huskers team had. On the field everyone knew Frazier was one of the program's leaders, even though he didn't have a "C" on his jersey. "You also got to remember there were a lot of other really good football players on that team as well," Peter said. "You can't necessarily look at one of the other captains and say, 'Well, he didn't deserve it.' Being a leader or being a captain, maybe when you break it all down, it can look a little different than just being a great leader on the field. Tommie was the guy that when a play needed to be made or, when things maybe didn't look like all sunshine and roses and everything, he was a guy that was going to just ram that offense down the field and he was going to make a play. When a play needed to be made, he was going to make it. It's one of, I think, life's greatest mysteries sometimes when talking about Nebraska football with Tommie not being voted a captain on offense."

Scott Frost, though, was also a national championship quarterback and a two-year starter who was not voted a captain in 1997, and Brown said he still uses the example of Frazier not being voted a captain today. Brown has worked on staff at NU for Osborne, Frank Solich, Bo Pelini, Frost, and now Matt Rhule. Frazier was a two-time national champion quarterback and the MVP of three different national championship games. "He's one of the top players in the last 50 years," Brown said. "I don't know whatever it is or whatever award you got, but it's true. He's one of the greatest players in the history of college football. He may be the greatest player who didn't win a Heisman in college football. For this guy not to be a captain shows you that he probably wasn't really well-liked, but you had to admit, and I think everybody—and this is why I tell people as an inspiration—I say, 'Look, Tommie Frazier wasn't elected as the captain on our team, but everybody knew when we hit that field who the real leader was on our team.' We all knew who the captain was on the team. He may not have won the vote, but he clearly was the leader. That's a great message for all our players because we're always looking for some type of kudos or some type of thing that we can honor ourselves with and so forth. It's a great privilege to be a captain, to be selected by your teammates as a captain, but who are you when your teammates don't select you as a captain because they maybe don't like your personality? Who are you then? Are you a guy that just goes in the tank? Are you a guy that's just going to try to please everybody and maybe regain it for the next year or what have you? It's not like that. Tommie Frazier was like: *You know what? You don't want to select me as captain. That's fine. I'm still going to lead this football team. It ain't going to matter whether you got the vote or not.* I think it's a great lesson for all of us."

The Heisman snub of 1995 was also one of college football's bigger mysteries, especially after Frazier's dominant performance in the Fiesta Bowl against Florida. Frazier rushed for 199 yards and two touchdowns with 105 yards passing and one touchdown through the air. Ohio State's Eddie George won the award in 1995 over Frazier. "It was really a shame that he didn't win the Heisman in '95 because, I think, if the voting had been after the bowl game—we beat Florida rather badly—he had a great game," Osborne said. "If the voting had occurred after the last game, which it seems to me would make sense—they still want to do it in fairly early December for some reason. That bowl game at the end of the year is really sometimes the most important game that you play. Anyway, I think he finished second and I've always been sorry that he didn't win it."

Winning the Heisman would've been a great honor for Frazier, but as Brown said, he doesn't need an award or title to feel accomplished. He let his play on the field do the talking. "I don't know to what degree that motivated Tommie for that Fiesta Bowl game. I do know this though. This is what I honestly believe. Even if Tommie Frazier had won the Heisman Trophy, and that was underneath him now as he got ready for that bowl game, I think he would've played with the same vigorous intent," Brown said. "I just didn't see him being a very circumstance-based player. I saw him being a circumstance-free player...I think the average man would've felt like, *Wow, man, it seems like I should have won it.* We had clearly a dominant team, and he had a great year. Maybe that was a little extra mustard on the hot dog. Maybe that was, but I don't think we would have seen a much less motivated Tommie Frazier even if he had won the Heisman, to be honest with you."

What's interesting about that 1996 Fiesta Bowl game against Florida is Frazier arguably delivered his Heisman moment. In NU's 62–24 win against the Gators, Frazier broke seven tackles and dodged two defenders on his 75-yard touchdown run that is the most defining play of the Osborne era. Brown finds himself rewatching that play even to this day. "I actually watched it today believe it or not, not knowing that I was going to talk to you about this," Brown told me. "You learn something new each time. Obviously, that was one of the great runs in the history of college football. I looked at the rest of the players in that game. Clinton Childs is the tailback on that play. Tommie turned up the field, and Clinton was originally the pitchman, but Tommie didn't pitch it to him because the defense didn't allow Clinton to receive the pitch. Clinton just played it out up the field. He ends up coming back while Tommie was in the midst of that pack of guys where it looked like, oh, they probably got him now. Clinton comes in and blocks the guy, slams the guy that would have been a key guy to make the play. Reggie Baul is down there, fighting his tail off to block downfield. You have these linemen that are [still blocking]; everybody's still playing. Now, we're thinking maybe the play is over, but you still have some key guys that are blocking. That's my point. My point is that Tommie Frazier rubbed off—and I'm not saying it's all Tommie Frazier. It's a combination of Coach Osborne, the culture that was built, but we had the perfect quarterback for that culture. We really did. That was maybe the most dominant team in the history of college football. I'm not sure we would have been without Tommie Frazier."

10

2000s Legend: Ndamukong Suh

You can trace Ndamukong Suh's recruitment to Nebraska back to 2003 at Mississippi State. The late John Blake was in his first coaching gig after being fired as Oklahoma's head coach in 1998. Blake was always known as a great recruiter. Nearly all the key players on Bob Stoops' 2000 national championship team were Blake recruits. He knew how to connect with players, families, and people. Who knew that his initial connection with MSU soccer player Ngum Suh, Ndamukong's sister, would start a relationship that would ultimately deliver the most decorated defensive player in Nebraska school history. "He knew about me three or four years before he actually started recruiting me," Suh said on a podcast interview with ESPN's Ryen Russillo. "I would go down to Mississippi State in the summer and spend like two or three weeks with her. It shows you how small the world was from that standpoint."

Blake would leave Starkville, Mississippi, after one season and join Bill Callahan's staff at Nebraska in 2004. Callahan was very close with national recruiting expert Tom Lemming. He picked his brain on who were some of the top recruiters he could add to his first Huskers staff.

Blake's name was at the top of the list. In the Internet era of Nebraska football, Callahan's 2005 recruiting class delivered two eventual Big 12 Players of the Year and is the highest ranked in modern-day history.

Blake was a big part of it. In 2005 he beat USC's Pete Carroll head to head for five-star running back Marlon Lucky from Hollywood, Oklahoma for four-star linebacker Phillip Dillard from Tulsa, and Tennessee for Nashville defensive end Barry Turner. All three programs were national powers that didn't lose out on top in-state talent often. Blake was the X-factor. However, his biggest score that year was Suh. The Portland, Oregon, native committed to NU in January of 2005. He also took official visits to Nebraska, California, Miami, Mississippi State, and Oregon State.

It was Blake's ability to connect with Suh that won him over. "He would always come in and say, 'You are my freak. You are my No. 1 guy. You've got to come to Nebraska.' He would literally go to every single basketball and football game throughout my senior year," Suh said. "He would just build a relationship with my family and he was super close with my coaches. He was like an uncle to me. I had a great time of getting to know him through that recruiting process."

The interesting thing about Suh's journey to Nebraska is things didn't begin to take off for him until his fourth season. In today's immediate gratification world, recruits of Suh's caliber expect to play on Day One. Suh instead battled injuries and learned from future NFL draft picks like Adam Carriker, Jay Moore, and Stewart Bradley about what it took to play at this level.

Callahan would eventually be fired after the 2007 season, and Blake left Lincoln for North Carolina, following the 2006 season. The Nebraska program, which Suh signed with,was now much different. Gone was his original coaching staff, and in came Bo Pelini. Before Pelini had a chance to talk to Suh, he was highly considering leaving NU.

His meeting with Pelini changed everything and helped develop him into one of the best defensive players we have ever seen. "I give a huge amount of credit to Bo Pelini and his brother Carl Pelini," Suh said. "When Bo came to Nebraska, he was like, 'You are 10 times better than Glenn Dorsey. You are more athletic. I just need you to commit to the way I want to do things and how I want to run a defense.' I was like I am probably going to go back home to Oregon State and be more comfortable around home. Something told me after talking to my parents: let's not do that. Let me stick this out. There's a reason why I chose Nebraska. I decided to stay and then through that offseason and then going into the 2008 season, where I had torn my ACL in winter conditioning, I couldn't practice during spring ball, I couldn't do camp, I couldn't do anything. I owe Mark Mayer, who was the athletic trainer there at the time, a ton of credit. He came from the league, and he was with Callahan at the Raiders. He was like, 'I'm going to make sure you are fit and ready to go when it's time for Week One. You just have to trust me on this particular piece.'

"I said, 'Cool, I'm good from an athletic perspective in getting healthy, but how am I going to get immersed into this new system? I can't even practice.' Carl Pelini pulled me into his office, and I would just sit in there and learn every single position outside of my own position and how everything fit together. Once I did that, that opened my eyes up where I could find ways to cheat.

"Carl was like, 'I will never be mad at you if you cheat, but if you don't make the play, I'm going to dog cuss you out.'

"I was like, 'Perfect.'"

At the beginning of November 2008, it wasn't even a sure thing Suh was set to be named first-team All-Big 12. Then a lightbulb came on, and over the last few games of the 2008 season, Suh showcased the type of player he would become. The ACL injury he was coming off of during the winter of 2008 made his end-of-season results that much more impressive. "Maybe seven months is the earliest you can come back, but it's not going to be right away that the guy's going to be as good as he was," offensive line coach Barney Cotton said. "Suh came back and he only practiced once a day of the two-a-days, but he came back in four-and-a-half months from his ACL. Nobody does that. That gave me a first impression that this guy must have one hell of a constitution to be able to come back after an ACL. He was good at the beginning of that junior year, but he improved throughout that junior year because he was great by the end of that junior year. Even then, that was only eight months after an ACL injury, which is absolutely incredible. Then, obviously his senior year, it was out of this world."

The early film Pelini and his staff watched on Suh from 2006 and 2007 showed flashes of greatness, but still nobody could've predicted what he'd be like by the end of 2009. That season was as much a product of Suh buying in as anything. "Right when we got there, the first thing Bo wanted to do was break down film," former secondary coach Marvin Sanders said. "We had our video people make not really a highlight but a reel of all the returning players that had played a significant amount of time. As we watched that tape, we saw that he had some talent, but there was no way of us knowing he was going to be that. Then, when you watched him during spring practice and watched his work ethic over the summer time, you knew you had a chance of having something special."

Cotton also said the toughness Pelini's teams practiced with each day played a factor in getting the best out of Suh. "We had some real scuffles. Ricky Henry is one of the absolute toughest— if not the toughest—offensive linemen I ever coached," Cotton said. "As luck would have it, every time one's went against one's, it was Ricky against Suh, and those were epic battles. Because there were times when Ricky would really get after big Suh, and there were times obviously that Suh would get after Ricky. When those two guys got to go against each other, I know Ricky was All-Big 12 and everything, but he obviously didn't have the notoriety that Ndamukong did. Those were some serious battles those two guys had. The good thing about it is that I think that Suh was a great player because he was also a good practice player. Guys that work hard in practice that are great players mean a lot to me because—I shouldn't say that all great players don't—but he was a good practice player, not just a gameday player. He had a good work ethic."

Former Huskers quarterback Joe Ganz played with Suh at NU from 2005 to 2008. Ganz started quarterback for the final part of 2007 and the 2008 seasons. Suh was a hard person to get close to. He kept a small circle in the locker room but eventually began to warm up to some of the older players in the program. "He was the biggest freak athlete I've ever been around in terms of size, strength, agility," Ganz said. "When I was most in awe of him was when we first played pickup basketball on Saturdays. We would always go Saturday during the offseason, Saturday afternoon, early afternoon, and we played basketball before we'd all go out together Saturday night and we'd all play basketball. We'd always invite him and we'd try to get him to open up to us, but he's calculated in who he lets in and who he doesn't, right? He's always been like that whether it's business, football, whatever it is. He was just calculated who he let in. We wanted to make him a part of our thing, and I wanted him to be close to us, and finally he started opening up and he'd come with us. I remember the first day I watched him play basketball. I was like, *Holy shit.* I don't even think we're the same. I know we're both human beings, but we're not the same species. That was the first time where I was like, *Holy cow, this kid, he's not normal.* Then, you throw on just how intense he played the game, and it just added on to what he was as a football player and just how smart he was in terms of, not only just off the field, but how smart he was in terms of his football IQ.

"I know he would credit coach Bo and Carl with a lot of his development. I tell people all the time. They always want to ask like, 'Was he an asshole? Was he mean?' I was like, 'No, as long as he liked you, you were good.' He was the most physically gifted human being I've ever seen in terms of size, strength, speed, agility, football IQ. It was off the charts. You could just tell, but it was really the first time we played pick-up basketball together, where I was like, *Oh, wow.* That's not normal for the things he was doing on a basketball court."

By the end of 2008, Suh helped Pelini's team beat Colorado in Lincoln, Nebraska, and secure a spot in the Gator Bowl to face Dabo Swinney's Clemson squad. In a nationally televised New Year's Day game on CBS, Suh dominated as the Huskers beat the Tigers 26–21. The nation began to take notice of No. 93. "That was a really talented team that we played against," former defensive line coach John Papuchis said of Swinney's first Clemson team in 2009. "That was also, in my opinion, a little bit of a national coming out for Suh because I thought he really dominated that football game, and we knew how good he was, and he had showed flashes of being that guy. I don't know that it had shown on the national stage to that extent as it did on a New Year's Day game like that."

Papuchis has worked under Bo Pelini, Nick Saban, Les Miles, Kirby Smart, and Will Muschamp in his defensive coaching career. He knew what top-level talent looked like, especially after being a part of the 2007 LSU staff that won the national championship. They knew Suh's potential, but nobody could've predicted he would be this caliber of player. "We had just come from LSU, where we had some guys that were really good players, and signed Glenn Dorsey and Kyle Williams, and they had Tyson Jackson playing on the edge," Papuchis said. "We had been with some guys who were really good ones. Then, to see Suh once he was able to get healthy and you were like, *Wow, this guy could be different.* He was so athletic and he was so big and he was so smart. To have all those things in one player was—that doesn't happen very often. It obviously is why he was able to have the success that he had, do things that he did. I was in a high school recently and I was telling the coach about, 'Who would've ever thought that if you're coaching defensive line, you'd be at the Heisman Trophy finals?' With Suh we were at the finals for the Heisman and we might not see those things happen very often anymore."

So much of the legacy of Suh at Nebraska was built on the 2009 season. Suh could've gone pro after 2008 and probably been a late first-round pick. He chose to come back as a fifth-year senior. The decision paid off for everyone. Suh was a part of the last year before the NFL changed its rookie wage scale.

He was picked No. 2 in the 2010 draft by the Detroit Lions and earned more than $64 million in his first five seasons as a pro. When the rookie wage scale changed in 2011, the No. 1 pick, Cam Newton, received just $22 million over his first four NFL seasons. Suh's career earnings as a pro topped $168 million—the most ever for a Huskers players in the NFL. He's also one of the highest-paid defensive players in NFL history. "I remember basically Bo and Carl sitting down with him and talking to him about coming back and the value of another year and being a leader," Sanders said. "He didn't want to let his teammates down or the fans. He thought, *I can go make a lot of money.* But he literally loved Nebraska, his teammates, and that school. That's why he came back to school. We talked him into it. The state of Nebraska as a whole is what brought Ndamukong Suh back."

You can argue his value to Nebraska was much greater. Suh's 2009 season elevated the program's profile when conference realignment began. After the Huskers lost to Texas 13–12 in the Big 12 title game, Suh captured the nation. Nebraska looked to be back as a national power as more than 12 million people watched Suh and the Huskers nearly take down Texas. Only the BCS title game (17.2 million) and the Rose Bowl (13.2 million) drew higher ratings that season.

Suh finished fourth for the Heisman in one of the closest races ever. He picked up 161 first-place votes. Winner Mark Ingram received 227, runner-up Toby Gerhart received 222, and third-place finisher Colt McCoy received 203 votes. Suh finished ahead of Florida quarterback and 2007 Heisman winner Tim Tebow and he arguably stripped the Heisman away from McCoy after what he did to him the week before in the Big 12 title game. "His desire to finish his degree, coupled with the fact that I think he felt like he had more to achieve, he was very wise in his decision that his best ball was still ahead of him after his junior year," Papuchis said. "He made a really good financial decision by coming back, too, and giving himself that opportunity."

By the spring of 2010, conference realignment had begun. Nebraska received an invite to the Big Ten largely due to how attractive its football program looked at that time, coming off the 2009 season fueled by Suh. Pelini had NU on a trajectory to be a national power again, and the Big Ten jumped on the chance to add the Huskers. Looking at things now, who knows where Nebraska might be if not for the 2009 season. "It's surreal thinking back at it," Papuchis said of Suh's run in 2009. "Obviously, things were good from the standpoint that we had started to really turn the corner. [We] had a very disappointing loss to Texas in the Big 12 Championship Game, but you still felt optimism and excitement about where the program was heading toward. It was just a whirlwind of coming off of the championship game and then being out recruiting and then getting on the plane and going to the Heisman. Then, we flew right back immediately. That was no easy flight from New York back to Nebraska at 11:00 at night or midnight, whenever it was, because we had the bowl game to start getting ready for. I just remember it being an exciting time because you could feel like we were really turning the corner but almost probably in hindsight took it for granted a little bit because when you're young you think those things are going to happen, but you don't always realize how significant the moment was while you're in it."

Rick Kaczenski never coached Suh at Nebraska but replaced Carl Pelini as the Huskers' defensive line coach following the 2011 season. He said Suh's 2009 season added so much value on the recruiting trail when he recruited defensive linemen for the Big Red. "The guy's a living legend. I had all sorts of questions from the other coaches about him," Kaczenski said of Suh. "He changed the entire defense. You talk about a guy making people better. You're talking about a guy that struck fear in opponents. There aren't many guys that strike fear. Ndamukong Suh struck fear in every single offensive lineman, every single running back, every single quarterback that he played against. You just don't have that. You look at the defensive line that Nebraska has had, *holy cow*. You go look up those names sometimes in Memorial Stadium, and I know Randy's name isn't up there either, but you guys have had generational talent there. Nebraska had the best defensive lineman that has played in the history of the game. That's our opinion. Now, I didn't have the privilege of coaching him, but that's how Ndamukong is viewed…We used him in recruiting all the time. Man, 'Hey, Maliek [Collins], man, this is how I see you.' We put Suh tape on, showed these guys how they play. What I love about Suh is he's a great dude. He's a dude, just loves football and loves Nebraska."

If Nebraska had beaten Texas in the 2009 Big 12 title game, its reward would've been a trip to the Fiesta Bowl to play either Boise State or TCU. Instead, the Huskers landed in the Holiday Bowl and dominated Arizona 33–0. Sonny Dykes' offense, led by quarterback Nick Foles, was helpless. Arizona was the runner-up of the Pac-10 Conference and had just beaten Carroll's USC team to close the season. "That team would've had a chance to be in a 12-team playoff. We were better at the end of the season than we were at the start," Papuchis said. "You think about that Texas game obviously. [That] was the No. 2 team in the country, and we gave them every bit of what all they could handle. Then, obviously, what we did to Arizona at the bowl game, which was total domination. I think that team was just getting better as we were going on. If they had expanded playoff back then and we were able to get into it, that would've been a dangerous team to have to play against."

In 2009 Suh was named the AP College Football Player of the Year, winning the Outland Trophy and the Lombardi, Bronko Nagurski, Chuck Bednarik, and Bill Willis awards. He's the most decorated defensive player in program history and he's had arguably the best pro career for a Huskers defensive player.

The question is where does Suh rank all time. He never won a national title or even a conference championship. However, it's hard not to argue he's the greatest defensive player in school history. "He's in the group that you consider the best. It's always hard. I don't like to say this guy is one, this guy is two," former Huskers All-American and defensive lineman Jason Peter said. "You get to a certain level; you're in the upper echelon of Nebraska football players. That's where Ndamukong is. People got to remember he's a perfect example of what I was talking about before. He's a guy who comes in, I think, he—what—maybe played a few games but then had injuries or redshirts or something but doesn't really start to do something, really start to do something till about halfway through his junior year, and the light then goes on. Then, it's just like this thing is unleashed, this monster that just tears through anything and everything that gets in his way...Without Ndamukong in the 2008 and 2009 seasons, it's probably not as productive of a year for Nebraska football as it is with him. I feel like I was a tiny little piece in helping him get to that success. Him and I, we would talk on a kind of a regular basis, starting in his junior year, but watching him just become the player, yes, it was special. He's a once-in-a-generation type player to be able to be that size and be able to move the way that he did. You don't find many guys like that. You really don't. At a time when Nebraska football needed something to rally around, he was leading the charge."

PART 3

THE TRADITIONS

11

The Sellout Streak

No METRIC DEFINES NEBRASKA FOOTBALL MORE THAN ITS famed sellout streak. By the end of the 2024 season, it surpassed 400 games. (Major college football teams generally play seven home games per season.) The next longest one in college football history was Notre Dame, which saw its streak snap at 273 games during the 2019 season. The Irish's streak started in 1973, while the Huskers' goes back to 1962.

The streak is so much more than football. It's about pride. It's about a state getting together every fall Saturday rain or shine. There is nothing like it in the world in terms of fan support. The stadium seats around 90,000, and the state's population is 1.964 million. That means about one out of 22 people in the state of Nebraska occupy Memorial Stadium on gameday Saturdays. Only West Virginia (1.783 million) has a smaller population of the schools that make up college football's major conferences.

The streak is a measurement of the great fan support. It's that fan support that allows Nebraska to be in the Big Ten and generate top national television ratings each week despite the lack of success the program has seen on the field in recent years. "If you look at Nebraska football the last few years, we haven't had a whole lot to be proud of in terms of record on the field, bowl games, rankings," former head coach and athletic director Tom Osborne said. "The one thing that I think really has stood out is the loyalty of the fans. To me it would be unheard of that you go through five straight losing seasons or something like that and still have a sellout—99 percent of the football programs in the country, you'd have half-empty stadiums I would think. The sellout streak is big in recruiting because players know that when they come here they're going to be appreciated and they're going to be supported by the fanbase and the state. That's something that we certainly are very proud of."

The remarkable thing is that it doesn't matter if Nebraska is playing Ohio State or Idaho State. The stadium remains full, and the tickets are sold. The streak is the only thing that links all the eras of Nebraska football together—from Bob Devaney in 1962 to the present day. "You can't buy a ticket on gameday. There's no ticket booth in Lincoln at Memorial Stadium," former Nebraska assistant coach and Iowa State head coach Jim Walden said. "They have will call and they got places where the players' parents can pick up a ticket. You can't literally. There's no place to buy a ticket in Lincoln at Memorial Stadium. You should see the looks on some people's faces. They can't. It's like, *What?* It is unique. I don't know that there's any other stadium. I know there's nobody, no other stadium that's had a run that long. Now maybe Ohio State today, you may not be able to buy a ticket at the game. That wasn't necessarily the case when Woody Hayes was there. Ohio State would be the best choice you might have or maybe Michigan. That would be my guess that those two schools probably would be the most competitive two schools that could be said, 'How long has it been since you sold a ticket at your stadium?' I have no idea, but I know Alabama took a shot. They had their downtime. Texas has had some downtimes. LSU, you might have to check that out. I don't know that, but when you stop and try to think of the top five programs in the country that would have something that could be comparable, I'll bet you they haven't. I just think that's a record that's going to stand forever."

Nebraska football and simply filling Memorial Stadium with nearly 90,000 fans gives this state an identity. "They're proud of it. They're proud of their university," Walden said. "They're also supportive. It's their only school. It's their only Division I football team, and the big word is *only*...If you're living in Grand Island or Hastings or Omaha or wherever, the center point [is] for college football. You may love the University of Nebraska. Let's say the University of Nebraska-Omaha or Creighton. You may love Creighton basketball and you just love it with a passion. You also love Big Red football. There is no reason why anybody in Nebraska wouldn't love Nebraska football."

One of the key pieces to Nebraska's success was the players understanding the fan support. It's moving to see how much Huskers football means to people and how many people are willing to build their lives around football Saturdays. In Nebraska you don't schedule your wedding on a gameday Saturday. If somebody does, it turns into a Huskers watch party. Former All-American defensive lineman Jason Peter marvels at the appreciation from the fans. "It's amazing," he said. "You still go out in a small town of Nebraska, and they still live and die for it. It's what makes Nebraska special. It's not just the team you choose. It's this way of life almost. A lot of them identify, especially small towns, through Nebraska football. It was a prideful thing. They wear their Husker shirt when they go on vacation somewhere. It was like, 'Hey, I'm a Husker. You see all this gear I got on? I'm a Husker fan.' And they hoped that they run into another Husker fan. They're so proud of who they are. When you hear the stories of families, that second mortgage their home and stuff like that in order to get season tickets, or the stuff that they sacrifice in order to make it down there to Lincoln on Saturdays, it's like how can you even think about not giving everything you have to this program? It was another driving force knowing the support that we had. Coach Osborne and Coach McBride constantly reminded us of that. I felt Coach Osborne or Coach McBride always had a way of saying this. 'Remember who you are and play for your teammates and your brothers and play for your parents and your siblings.' He said, 'Most of all, you play for those fans because without them none of this is possible.' We were constantly reminded of it every single day."

When former Huskers play-by-play announcer and Nebraska historian Jim Rose thinks of Nebraska fans, the 2002 Rose Bowl in Pasadena comes to mind. That was the last time NU played for a national championship, as it fell to Miami 37–14 in front of a sold-out crowd of 93,781. More than 60,000 Nebraska fans filled the Rose Bowl in support of their team playing nearly 1,500 miles away from Lincoln. "I remember the Rose Bowl when we played Miami. This was my thinking when I looked out across that magnificent huge stadium, the greatest cathedral in college football," Rose said. "Two-thirds of it was Nebraska. Two-thirds of it was red, as I turned to the guy next to me. We were watching the game from the end zone. I said, 'This is the culmination of the greatest two generations in college football history. This right here is the ultimate culmination of Nebraska's dominance. Starting in 1962 with the sellout streak through all the conference championships, the five national titles, the 10 national title games, and here we are on the greatest stage in college football, primetime, tens of millions of people are going to watch Nebraska play for another national championship in the Rose Bowl.'

"I got to thinking this is something else. Now little did we know that this would be the end, that this would be the last thing for 20-some years now, but it was just an unbelievable picture. There's the Nebraska Cornhusker marching band on the field of the Rose Bowl in Pasadena, preparing for the national championship game, the 10th one in Nebraska's history. I just looked at myself and I thought how great it is to be in Nebraska, how wonderful it is to be a Husker fan. That was my feeling that here we are celebrating us. This incredible tradition, this remarkable passion, this love of place, this pride of place, and we're putting it on display for the whole country in the Rose Bowl game. I thought, *Man, some people are born lucky, and some people make their own luck.* But to be a Nebraskan on that night before kickoff of course was something special. We had the Heisman Trophy winner at quarterback, and we just thought, *We're going to win another one, man. We're going to do it again.*"

* * *

The genius of the Nebraska sellout was arguably the late Don "Fox" Bryant. He was Bob Devaney's right-hand man and NU's media relations director. His ability to promote NU was significant over the years. From producing the first media guides to send to recruits to using color photos in those guides, Bryant knew how to sell Nebraska. He knew which reporters to call and who to talk to when things needed to get done.

In 1962 when NU recorded its first sellout, it was Bryant who immediately started tracking it as a streak. That foresight by Bryant/Nebraska to keep proper records on something so significant helped make the streak what it became. Other schools like Ohio State may have been selling out their games, but they were not properly recording and tracking. Nobody in 1962 could have had any idea in 2024 how big this would become. "Don Bryant was as much a part of the success of Nebraska football as anybody off the field," Huskers historian Jim Rose said. "He was absolutely the preeminent public relations personality of his time, and it's one of the reasons why he had a world of friends, and he was always involved in major sports events like the Super Bowl or the Olympic Games because people loved having Don Bryant around. Fox knew he had a guy in Bob Devaney who was like him that loved people and loved building relationships. He and Devaney were coconspirators in building this national brand, and at the same time, television came to college sports. They come into Lincoln in the '60s and beamed games across the country, and Fox said, 'I can build a national brand for Husker football.' And he did because you had a coach who never turned down an interview, slapped backs with every reporter back in the days when you could do that. They were all World War II veterans. You had a perfect mix of a PR guy and a coach who was PR sensitive to help build Nebraska football."

Tom Osborne also understands the significance of the streak, and some of Nebraska's early steps led by Bryant played a big factor in laying the groundwork for where it's at today.

"It's certainly an important record," Osborne said. "We kept track of it. It's been a big thing."

Osborne was at that first sellout on November 3, 1962, against Missouri. The Huskers lost that day 16–7 in a game televised on CBS. The sold-out crowd of 36,000 set the stage for future renovation projects to Memorial Stadium that brought the capacity to more than 90,000 by 2013. Memorial Stadium went from a seating capacity of 31,000 in 1962 to more than 70,000 by 1972. The original stadium only had seating on the east and west sides. A four-series project that began in 1964 enclosed the stadium by adding seats above the north and south end zones, which brought the capacity to 74,000. In 1999 NU added skyboxes and club seating on the west side to bring the capacity to 78,000. In 2006 Nebraska expanded its seating in the north end zone and added more skyboxes to bring the capacity to more than 85,000. In 2013 NU added skyboxes, club seating, and another balcony to bring the stadium capacity to 91,000.

The stadium has come a long way since its first sellout in 1962. "It was a Missouri game, and I remember that game," Osborne said. "It was a hard-hitting game. They had physically talented players, and it was really a very physical game… It was Bob's first year. We'd won a couple early in the year, and momentum began to build because I remember when I was in junior high school probably when I went to my first Nebraska game and I sat down in the knothole section. They had bleachers at both ends of the field. I think it cost 50 cents or something like that to get in. I went to a game or two there. Then I had an uncle that had four seats up in the main stadium and I went to a couple of games with him. I would say at that time, I think the stadium seated just over 35,000, and there were games where there wouldn't have been over 20,000 there. Then, of course, once Bob came and started winning, we closed in the south end zone first. They built the stadium at the south end. At that time we had a track around the football field, and that's where track meets were run. It's interesting because these players were disappearing in the stands when we were running a quarter or a half mile, whatever. Then when they filled in the north end, I think then they figured a way they couldn't really continue to do that. So they moved the track down to where it is now from where it was. I think '65 was the year they filled in the south end. The north end zone was a couple of years later."

When Devaney took the job at Nebraska, he knew the potential of the fanbase. It was a sleeping giant. "My dad always felt that. I remember [Michigan State head coach] Duffy Daugherty had told him that if you win, you're going to have the support of the state," Mike Devaney said. "My dad really worked that, too. They were the only state institution or only basically game in town for the whole state. I think he tried to really play on the fact that, 'Hey, this is your university. We need your support. With your support we can win.' I think it all came to fruition and I think he felt that that was extremely important as a part of Nebraska's history and their success over the years because of the fan support and because it was the only game in town, and the people supported it unbelievably."

What's equally impressive about the Nebraska sellout streak is it doesn't just stay in Lincoln. No fanbase travels like Huskers fans. That started in the Big 8 when locals had a better chance of landing tickets to a game in Lawrence or Manhattan, Kansas; Columbia, Missouri; Boulder, Colorado; or Ames, Iowa; than in Lincoln. "They couldn't get tickets to home games. It was for all those fans who couldn't get tickets to home games," Rose said. "For a long time in the '70s, there was a waiting list, a season-ticket waiting list that numbered into 10,000 to 12,000. Nobody gave up their seats when there are only two or three football games on TV every year, and not only that, but

Husker football was not a year-round thing. Like now where you can go on social media, you can go on Internet sites now and you can gorge yourself on Nebraska football 365 days a year. You can look at recruiting film, game film, old games, old interviews. So there really was a lot of pent-up demand for the product, and thousands and thousands of Nebraskans could not get tickets to home games. They would buy three games a year—KU, K-State, Iowa State, Missouri, once in a while Colorado, once in a while Oklahoma State and they would get a chance to see their favorite team and they would just take over the stadium. It was really amazing. It was a migration."

Then in 1976 the power of the Nebraska fans was on full display. The Huskers played a game in Honolulu against Hawaii to close out the regular season, and it resulted in something unprecedented. "This is a fanbase that in 1976 sent 25,000 people to Hawaii for a football game," Rose said. "It was the largest person-to-place airlift in U.S. aviation history at that time. This is a fanbase that looked at Husker football as a great road trip regardless of where it was.

"I just remember Don Bryant saying we are now approaching the Berlin Airlift numbers for this 1976 Hawaii game because the weather was terrible, and we just had one jumbo jet after another taking off from the Lincoln Municipal Airport and landing in Honolulu because 25,000 Husker fans were carried from Nebraska to the islands for one football game."

Over the years more than 25,000 Nebraska fans have made road trips to USC (2006), Washington (2010), UCLA (2012), and Oregon (2017). All four of those teams are now in the Big Ten, and you can expect that to continue. When Nebraska first joined the Big Ten in 2011, the Big Red made its first road trip to Northwestern the following season in 2012. That will go down as one of the bigger fan flexes, as it sent a message to the entire Big Ten how passionate Nebraska fans are. Nebraska occupied more than two-thirds of Ryan Field in Evanston and witnessed a comeback win, in which the Huskers were down 12 points in the fourth quarter. The crowd noise got so loud for the Wildcats that they were forced to operate on a silent snap count in their own stadium. That is unheard of in college football. "I remember playing at Northwestern a couple of different times and just looking around and feeling like it was almost a home game atmosphere, which was pretty amazing," former defensive coordinator John Papuchis said. "It is one of those things where you never want to take it for granted, but it was such a good fanbase and such a great experience having the opportunity to play or coach for them and be around them. I think that the Northwestern game sticks out to me just because that was a place that didn't always pack with home fans, and all of a sudden, we just took it over. It was pretty special."

Former defensive line coach Rick Kaczenski remembers the optics of the Nebraska fans taking over the Northwestern stands. "I used a photo for recruiting," Kaczenski said. "At that point we were on the opposite sideline. We were away from the press box, and I know they changed that in the years after that, but our whole side and the press box side and the end zones had a bunch of red, and that was a tight game. I think we came back from 12 points down in that game, and it got loud when we needed it. Once again Northwestern had the ball, some opportunities to win, and the crowd affected it. For a crowd to affect a team on their home turf, that says a lot about your fanbase. Yes, that was cool. When we were recruiting a kid, I would say, 'Hey, check out this picture.' I would write a handwritten note on some stationery with that away crowd on it. That was pretty damn cool."

As former Huskers player Jimmy Burrow watched Nebraska from afar over the years, he was amazed at times seeing the support NU got on the road. "I always wondered how the other teams allowed that to happen, but it was always like that," Burrow said. "It was a big part of winning road games for us over the years. I'm not sure what the road record is, but back in the day, I know it was great because it was like still playing in front of a home crowd…Think about if 50,000 people are in a stadium and 15,000 to 20,000 are Nebraska fans. It doesn't seem like a home game to the home team really. That creates about as much momentum as you normally see when you walk into Nebraska."

One of the Huskers' last great stadium takeovers was in 2019 at Colorado when NU occupied more than 65 percent of CU's Folsom Field. Former athletic director Bill Moos joked after the game that he told Colorado AD Rick George that Nebraska fans helped pay the bills for the rest of his athletic programs that year. But soon Nebraska will have to foot the bill for stadium renovations.

Memorial Stadium turned 100 years old in 2023. The sell-out streak surpassed 400 games in 2024. The question now for athletic director Troy Dannen, who was named to his position in 2024, and his team is how they keep this streak going. The answer? Improving Memorial Stadium's overall fan experience like adding chairbacks, more premium seating options, alcohol sales, and better concession offerings. The up-and-coming generation of Huskers fans have not experienced much winning from Nebraska football. To engage this group of fans better, Nebraska will take on its biggest facility project yet—a complete renovation of Memorial Stadium. "We are going talk about a project that is the most complicated project we can undertake," former University of Nebraska president Ted Carter said in

September of 2022. "We literally are going to be repairing and rebuilding an airplane while we are flying it. I can understand that. In my own personal world, I rebuilt an aircraft carrier in 2006 for $2 billion that was already existing. This is not completely unlike that—except we are not replacing nuclear reactors."

Carter came to Nebraska as a former Navy admiral. He would eventually move on from NU to take the position of Ohio State president in 2024. Before Carter left, he and former athletic director Trev Alberts knew the challenges they faced to give Memorial Stadium the facelift it needs. It's unrealistic to think the next generation of Nebraska fans will continue to sit in 20-inch bench seats that don't have chairbacks. It's unrealistic to think that people will keep filling up the south end zone, which has not been renovated since being built in the 1960s. The south end zone is 98 rows with no escalators or concourses. Its only concession stands are located at ground level, and the bathroom facilities still feature horse trough style urinals. For many of the people, getting to their seats in the south stadium might be the most challenging fitness test they take on during the week. "We have a 100-year-old stadium that is iconic, that we love," Alberts said. "The reality is there has been so much change and so much technological change, and I think we are behind. I think we need to dive into how do we ensure that [for] the next 50 to 100 years of Memorial Stadium that that fan experience and that modernization is there."

Rose knows how much this project will end up costing, but if not done, the sellout streak will eventually end. It's been saved over the years by boosters who buy up last-minute unsold tickets. In 2021 Nebraska also started the Big Red Carpet Experience, a program where supporters purchase tickets for different youth organizations that may not be able to afford to attend a Huskers football game. It's been wildly successful, as thousands of youths in the state have been able to attend a Nebraska game.

Still, this is a short-term fix. The stadium will need proper upgrades to keep the streak alive in the long run. "The next generation's expectation is: I want a show," Rose said. "I want to be treated to a hell of a time. I want access to my favorite liquor or beverage. I want a comfortable seat. I want Wi-Fi that's uninterrupted. I want to be able to go in and watch other games at halftime or when the game's a blowout—one way or the other. I want a different experience because I'm used to a different experience, and that will make the stadium different. You'll still have a lot of seats for folks that don't want to do any of that, but I really like how they're thinking long term. How do we turn Saturdays from a football game into an experience, a killer experience? It's going to cost a little bit more. The average Husker is going to have to cut loose a little bit more to get that, but they'll come away thinking, *This is great. This is the thing I want. This is the thing I'll come back to.* And to a certain extent, it may not necessarily hinge on the outcome of the game. It may be, yes, the Huskers are in the Big Ten now. The Big Ten is like the AFC West, so the days of 13–0 are probably gone, but let's be in the hunt for the playoffs. Let's stay in the hunt. Let's win a big game here and there, but I don't expect a 13–0 season. I expect us to get into the playoffs. Well, that changes expectations dramatically."

12

The Blackshirts

Sometimes, the best traditions happen organically. One of the greatest traditions in Nebraska's football program is the historic Blackshirt practice jersey. The story of the Blackshirt is a simple one that took on a life of its own. In 1964 head coach Bob Devaney was looking for a way to designate his defensive units in practice when going against the offense, which wore a red practice jersey.

Tom Osborne, an assistant coach in 1964, still remembers when Devaney sent running backs coach Mike Corgan to a local Lincoln, Nebraska, sporting goods store to buy jerseys to help him better identify his defensive units in practice. "Mike Corgan was a backfield coach under Bob and Mike was in charge of buying equipment," Osborne said. "He went down to a place called Gary's Sporting Goods. They were going to use half jerseys. At that time we would have four offensive teams and four defensive teams. The question was: how are you going to distinguish when you're scrimmaging? He said he had some black half jerseys, and there were some green half jerseys, and there were yellow half jerseys, and then there was white. They used those half jerseys to distinguish defensively. The offense was always dressed in red jerseys when we scrimmaged like spring ball or fall camp or whatever. The first defense had black jerseys, second outfit had yellow, third had green, and the fourth had white. It was just an accidental thing, but, eventually, it got to be if you're a first-team player, you wear a Blackshirt. It just caught on. It wasn't anything intentional. We didn't think, *The 'Blackshirt' has a nice ring to it.* We didn't promote it. It just happened to be. It's how we distinguish one team from another."

From there it took on a life of its own mainly because of defensive coordinator Charlie McBride. He joined the staff in 1977 after Monte Kiffin and a few other assistant coaches moved on. Osborne met McBride for the first time at the American Football Coaches Association (AFCA) coaching convention in Miami. He was coaching at Wisconsin and before that he worked under Frank Kush at Arizona State. McBride would go on to have a 23-year career at NU from 1977 to 1999, serving as the defensive coordinator for 18 seasons. It was during that time that the standard of being a Blackshirt developed. "Charlie played on that, I think. Charlie was really a good coach," Osborne said. "I went to a coach's convention and met him and liked him. He coached for Frank Kush down at Arizona State as well, and Frank was really a tough guy. Charlie was a pretty tough coach. Sometimes we had to talk a little bit about how we would handle things, but he really became a great defensive coordinator."

In some ways McBride was the perfect counterbalance to Osborne. McBride had the ability to flip a switch, and the players fed off his intensity. He created a culture of toughness and accountability. It was player-led. The players set the standard of what it took to be a Blackshirt. "I just remember when my brother Christian would call home and talk about what was happening in the program. He'd always talk about these Blackshirts and how they rode," former All-American defensive lineman Jason Peter said. "It's just the meanest, toughest dudes on defense. It was what you strived to be as a player here. I don't know; it was like a special forces type unit. It's like being a SEAL out of the military. This was how you looked at the Blackshirts just among football players. It was like you were this elite unit. Chances were that if you wear a Blackshirt you probably were going to have a good chance of playing in the NFL someday...The guy that led the Blackshirts was demanding and could be hard on guys, but it was all part of the toughness that was being created out here in the program on defense."

Players like Christian and Jason Peter ultimately helped define the Blackshirts. They brought the intangibles to the locker room, eventually taking Osborne's program over the top.

They were a reflection of McBride and the standards he set. "The Peter brothers had an edge," former Huskers running back Tony Davis said. "You need to get guys who are almost criminals, but you can keep under control. Those are the kind of people you want on your team. You want those types of players that you have to kill them to beat them. If you don't kill them, you're going to get beat because these guys never give up."

* * *

In today's sports world, you might have parents attend college football practices, watch film, and even schedule meetings with the coaching staff to discuss their son's playing time. When Charlie McBride ran the defense at Nebraska, it was a different time. There was no social media, cell phones, or heavy parent involvement. Things were hard because that's how it was supposed to be. It was the culture McBride engrained to set the standard of what it meant to be a Blackshirt. "You didn't have to worry about guys running to the president and being the whistleblower," former Huskers defensive lineman Jason Peter said. "Not that it's the same stuff that went on at Northwestern. Yes, they had a little more freedom to speak their mind and say things and not have to worry about us obviously either telling somebody or going on social media, even telling your parents. Now there are stories of the parents sometimes way too over-involved and almost are kept up to date on the practice notes from their child. I mean, being on the staff [under Scott Frost] for a little bit in 2021 and 2022, I was able to get a real inside look at some of that stuff. Having moms and dads call your position coach, that stuff really wouldn't have flown with Charlie. Occasionally, you'd hear about maybe a parent that did call Charlie. The first thing that Charlie did was let everybody know that that player's parent called or something. He was probably running home to that parent and saying, 'I'm never going to tell you anything again. Don't you ever call coach McBride!' He just would never do that back then. Part of it was because the upperclassmen were so strong as leaders, and they'd also let you know that, 'Hey, this is part of the deal, right?' It's not the end of the world. It's just Charlie and, even though he will chew you out or something, he's the first guy that's going to put his arm around you and tell you, 'Hey, I'm just doing this for your best,' and it was just part of the deal. You just knew that you didn't run and tell somebody or you didn't turn Coach McBride in or Coach Steele or whoever it was."

Instead, McBride relied on players like Christian and Jason Peter to be the enforcers of the culture he wanted to instill. Things were player-led. This helped build some of the best defenses in college football and played a crucial part in Osborne's teams winning three national championships. "When Christian and Jason played together, what I was really worried about, and I mean really worried, is that they would get into a fight in the game on the field and blame one another for making a mistake," McBride said. "I remember one time in the back of a car they got into a fight, and Jason punched Christian and broke his nose, and they laugh about it. These guys were scary because they were competitive. Even in games when somebody gained a yard, they would get mad at one another. I thought they'd get into a fight on the field. They'd be yelling at each other in between plays and stuff like that. Christian was a leader. He was a grab-you-by-the-throat leader. Christian was maybe more so like that, but both of them where like that. Both down deep, they were going to do everything possible to win. I remember when we played Missouri and went into overtime, and we scored and we had to stop them. I'm standing on the sideline, and we have to stop them to win the game. I'm going to give a speech and I turn around and I'm looking right at Wistrom and Jason Peter. They ran right by me, and their eyeballs were as big as silver dollars. I was like, *And I'm going to give them some speech?* I just shut my mouth and let them go. The next thing you know, they were sacking the quarterback twice. There was no way they were going to beat us—absolutely none."

Since McBride's retirement following the 1999 season, every coach has done their best at Nebraska to carry on the tradition of the Blackshirts. The rule of thumb is that the week of the first game is when the Blackshirts are passed out. Under McBride there were generally just 11 handed out each year. "The top 11 guys got Blackshirts, and that's the way it went," McBride said. "We handed them out the Monday of the first game week.

Everybody would come down and see what was in their locker. Most of the guys would come down, and they pretty much knew who it was going to be. It was kind of an unwritten rule that there were only 11 of them given out, but as time went on, we might have three guys play equal at a position like defensive end. So we ended up maybe giving one to Mike Rucker, even though he wasn't actually a starter."

We've seen coaches do it ceremonially and have former Blackshirts return to be a part of it. Another way it's been done is just to have the jerseys hang in the players' lockers before practice. "They all have their own way of doing it. Some maybe don't want to do it as much, but I think it's part of Nebraska," Peter said of the Blackshirt tradition. "If Nebraska can finally get its head above water, I think it's one of the greatest traditions in college football—the Blackshirts. It's every bit as much like something for the fans to latch onto. When 80,000 people in Memorial Stadium are doing the Husker Power or watching the tunnel walk, it's the Blackshirts as well."

Some coaches have used fewer than 11 Blackshirts over the years when position battles were still up for grabs. There have also been some years where more than 15 Blackshirts were passed out to avoid hurt feelings in the locker room. A few different NU coaches have taken away the Blackshirts after bad defensive performances. Former head coach Bo Pelini would even wait until after his team played what he considered the standard of Blackshirt defense before passing them out. There was a year the Blackshirts weren't passed out until November under Pelini.

The one thing that has gone away, which Jason Peter would like to see come back, is the tradition of having the second-team defense wearing gold jerseys. He always felt that was equally as important as passing out Blackshirts to let those players know how close they were to earning one. "You have to bring the gold shirts back as well," Peter said. "I'm pretty sure Bo didn't use gold shirts. I think the last person that used gold shirts was probably Frank [Solich]. Where the problem lies for me is that maybe you have 11 guys that are just Blackshirts and then what? Then everybody else falls into just the same grouping. It doesn't matter if you're second team or if you're fifth team—that's not reality. Fifth team isn't second team. I also think it lets you know where you stand. I think in order to know where you want to go, you got to know where you're starting as well, too. Being a gold shirt, you knew you were right on the cusp. It was a little more effort, a little more in the weight room, a little bit more studying the playbook, and then maybe one day, I'll have my Blackshirt. Should the fifth-string guy think he's on the same level as second-string guy? Hell no. The second-string guy is doing reps and playing in games. I think it just gives everybody else this relaxed feeling of like, *Well, there's no pressure.* The fans that have come in today or the people watching practice or whatever, they can't tell whether I'm second string or fifth string or sixth string or third string or whatever.

"I always thought that the gold shirts were just as big a part of what Nebraska's defense was as to what the Blackshirts was. Everything had a pecking order. It's kind of: *you're here, you're here, you're here, and you're here.* Now it's kind of just, *well, there's one guy here, and then everybody else just fits in.* What the heck is that? I wish that they would bring back guys that were on the third, fourth string, they wore red shirts—or whatever—white shirts. Then the second string, kind of maybe a few third stringers would wear gold shirts, and then you'd have the starters and maybe a few extras that wore Blackshirts. I think it's important to know where you stand on a daily basis. Those were jerseys that sometimes revolved on a daily basis. It was important, I think, and I think it's important in sports to know where you are."

Tampa Bay Buccaneers linebacker and former Huskers star Lavonte David is one of the current NFL defensive standouts, and being a part of the Blackshirt tradition has greatly impacted him. "It was a big deal. On my recruiting visit, everybody was talking about being a Blackshirt, what it takes to be a Blackshirt," the former All-American linebacker said during his NFL Combine draft interview in 2012. "The tradition of the Blackshirts goes way back, way back. You gotta earn it; you've gotta prove to the coaches that you're capable of getting the Blackshirt and to your teammates as well."

When Frost took over in 2018, he tried to bring as much of the Blackshirt tradition into the program as we've seen. Each year he had former Blackshirts come back to talk about the meaning of the jersey before presenting to each player. That is probably one of the most important elements of carrying on the tradition: educating each new group of Blackshirts on what it means to wear the practice jersey. "As Grant and Jason so eloquently stated: when they were here, the bar was set pretty high already," former defensive coordinator Erik Chinander said in 2018. "They knew how to operate. It's not quite like that right now. I want those guys to get a taste of what that standard is, what the bar is supposed to be, how you're supposed to act when you're a Blackshirt. I don't think the level of the upperclassmen and those types of things have been here the past few years. So I think it's important to get guys who were there when they were operating at the highest level to verbalize it [to] our guys."

13

The Walk-On Program

WHEN BOB DEVANEY TOOK THE WYOMING JOB IN 1957, THE state had a population of 314,000. He came from Michigan, which had a population of 7.57 million at the time. His Wyoming Cowboys needed to find a way to broaden their recruiting and turn over new stones. Devaney's idea: start a walk-on program. At that time taking walk-on players was unheard of for many reasons. Schools had virtually unlimited scholarship numbers, as it wasn't uncommon to be able to take around 50 recruits per year and have rosters of more than 200 players all on scholarship.

Jim Walden played for Devaney in 1958 and 1959 at Wyoming and later coached with him at Nebraska from 1969 to 1972. He remembers exactly how the walk-on program began for Devaney and how it later helped transform things at Nebraska. "Devaney endeared himself to the Wyoming people at that time," Walden said. "Then the next thing he did, he put out an all-points bulletin for walk-on kids to come to Wyoming, an open invitation. There were no limitations on how many you could have on the team at any one time. Knowing at that time Wyoming probably only had 300,000 people—and we used to say, 'There are more cows than there are people in Wyoming,'—it was a smart thing to do. They bought in. He just really worked hard with the locals, all the coaches in the state, to encourage any moderately good athlete to come down and take a chance. Through that we ended up with several really good Wyoming players that probably wouldn't have even gone to college to play ball had it not been for that invitation."

Former Huskers play-by-play voice and historian Jim Rose recalls an early story about the walk-on program under Devaney from former sports information director Don "Fox" Bryant.

"Don Bryant told me many stories about how he and Devaney would get in the car, drive down the interstate, and just appear at Rotary Club luncheons and Legion Club dinners and Kiwanis Clubs, and he would sell the program," Rose said. "He was a funny guy. He lit up the audience. They loved him. He had a great, great sense of humor and he was such a cheerleader. He said, 'Send me your guys, send me your best players, I'll put them on the field.' They did. That's what built the walk-on program and that's what built our program into success. Then after the '68 season when they went 6–4 and things fell apart, he knew things were good because he knew the material that was coming into the program."

What made it easy to walk on at places like Nebraska and Wyoming is that you didn't have other local competition in recruiting. There was no Football Championship Series (FCS) football back then. So it was quite a step down if you weren't playing Division I. Also, the cost of education was not as high. So many players could afford to bet on themselves. "Now walk-on programs in some states like Michigan might not be as appealing," Walden said. "In those days if they couldn't go to Michigan or Michigan State on scholarship, they went to Western Michigan or Eastern Michigan or wherever. Nebraska was unique in that it was the only major school in the state just like Wyoming. It wasn't hard to talk them into coming because you are the only Division I chance they would have."

Walden recalls that many of the early walk-on players for Devaney appreciated the opportunity they were getting. Many wanted a chance, and Devaney was willing to give them one. "The walk-on guys only got to eat the evening meal. They didn't get the other two. They got the walk-on evening meal, and hey, that was pretty good," Walden said. "You're getting a nice dinner every night, free. Then most of them if they were going to go to college, they were going to pay for it anyway. Why not give it a shot? Everything's furnished. You didn't have to furnish a damn thing to come out there as a freshman football player. All you had to pay for was your normal room, board, and books because you're paying your own way. Come out for football, and hey, it could lead to a scholarship. The worst it's going to do is you find out a year later you're not good enough, and you go on about your business."

Former Huskers linebacker and Wisconsin head coach Barry Alvarez would take Devaney's walk-on idea into his own program in Madison. Alvarez called the players "erasers," helping you compensate for recruiting misses. Walden agreed that the large walk-on classes made their job easier. "We had a philosophy," Walden said. "We didn't talk about it much, but we all knew it that there was no way in hell we were ever going to have a bad recruiting year. We could go out and give 32 full rides, but we're going to get 50 to 75 guys from Nebraska or maybe Kansas. We didn't know. But 90 percent of them were going to come from Nebraska. They were guys that wrestled from way out in the western part of the state. They played baseball, they played basketball, they played football. Take a 6'3", 217-pound guy. He knocks off the two sports he'd been playing, shows up at Nebraska in September. He's already up to 232 pounds. By the end of his first year, he's 241 pounds. He's 6'3½" at the time. He's running a 4.75 in the 40. He's a defensive end. First thing you know: 'Son of a bitch, where'd we get this guy?' You can't imagine how many good athletes we didn't recruit that ended up being great players for the University of Nebraska. That's why I knew we were never going to have a bad year recruiting because if the ones we recruited didn't turn out, the ones we didn't would."

Over the history of Nebraska's walk-on program, the success stories are undeniable. Twenty-five walk-ons have gone on to be future NFL draft picks. Seven went on to play for eventual Super Bowl teams. Linebacker Jimmy Williams out of Washington, D.C., wrote Tom Osborne a handwritten letter asking for an opportunity to play for the Huskers. He was NU's first walk-on to become a first-round NFL draft pick, and the Detroit Lions selected him in the 1982 NFL Draft. Williams went on to play 12 seasons in the NFL.

The boom of the walk-on program may have been from 1980 to 1985. During that time 10 former walk-on players were drafted into the NFL. NU's first ever walk-on drafted was tight end Jim McFarland in 1970 by the Arizona Cardinals. McFarland was an All-Big 8 tight end on NU's 1969 team that helped turn the corner for the Devaney era in Lincoln, Nebraska.

The late Milt Tenopir said the walk-on program was the infrastructure he needed to build some of the greatest offensive lines in college football history. "First of all we needed more linemen than most people practiced with," Tenopir said. "Probably half our guys up front were walk-ons, and we'd probably have 18 or 19 guys on scholarship, and 15 or 16 were walk-ons. When we did our walk-on recruiting, we looked for guys that hadn't been offered but had a legitimate chance of playing. As the years went on, the quality walk-on players kind of dwindled simply because of economic times. If a kid got a scholarship to South Dakota State or Kearney or UNO, it became hard to get them to walk-on. We had times that we probably didn't have the quality of walk-on kids that we needed to give us a good picture, and part of that was because of economic times. Education wasn't cheap. A lot of the quality walk-ons that we got back then may not have been offered by others back then, but they were good enough to take a shot on. A lot of them proved their worth.

"When we played Florida State one year in the 1994 Orange Bowl, we had a scholarship eight-man football left tackle Lance Lundberg from Wausa, and our left guard was a walk-on named Kenny Mehlin from Humboldt. Jim Scott was our center and he was a walk-on. He transferred from Kearney and was from the small town of Ansley, Nebraska. The entire left side of our line was made up of eight-man players, and only one of them was a scholarship guy. You can go back and find a bunch of guys like that. You had guys like Matt Hoskinson and Josh Heskew. Coach and I went down to an award ceremony in Oklahoma, and Josh and his dad brought a film with him, and I told Coach after watching it we could probably make a lineman out of him. We took him and made a great player out of him."

The walk-on program also was a key piece of building the culture and work ethic at Nebraska. When highly-recruited guys saw players, who may have never had a chance to see the field at NU, working hard, it forced them to work as hard or harder. "It's really important. It really is. It's something that [Osborne] believed in and it goes to kids that grew up watching Nebraska football," former walk-on offensive lineman Matt Hoskinson said. "You played football at a small-town Nebraska high school, and to have the opportunity to wear the Scarlet and Cream and just be a part of something that's been a part of your life for a long time is a really, really big deal. Milt and [Osborne] really loved guys that had chips on their shoulder. Maybe they were undersized, maybe they were 4.6 guys instead of 4.4 guys. The thing that you couldn't measure that an NFL Combine tries to measure is heart. That's what the walk-on program is built on. It's guys that play above their athletic ability and what it would allow them to play just because they are so thrilled to be a part of Nebraska's football program. There's hundreds and hundreds and hundreds of players that never saw significant playing time that meant something to the program, whether it be through practice or leadership or being a part of the scout team. There are more guys that you can possibly name off that were a huge part of the program."

Walden recalls that when he first got into college football, the thought of playing a walk-on or placing one on a scholarship was unheard of. He remembers the story of eventual All-Big 8 safety Jimmy Burrow. You might recognize the last name, as he's the father of 2019 Heisman Trophy-winning quarterback Joe Burrow.

Jimmy Burrow walked on to Mississippi and had a promising start to his young career. But because he was a walk-on, the coaching staff made it hard for him to advance in the program, which led him to Nebraska. "When I was a young kid in high school in Mississippi, you couldn't even walk on at the University of Mississippi," Walden, a Mississippi native, said. "If you didn't get a scholarship, you weren't allowed to even come down there. I think probably it was the same thing at Mississippi State and all those schools. I don't ever know why they didn't take walk-ons. Another thing—I'll never forget this—I recruited a young man named Jimmy Burrow from Amory, Mississippi. You might know that name. He's the father of Joe Burrow, which seems to be what his handle is these days. I coached him in high school, and he was now a freshman at Ole Miss, and I'm now at Nebraska, my first year. In 1970 he was a freshman at Ole Miss. I get a call from his dad and the freshman coach at that time. He had recommended Jimmy Burrow get a scholarship to the head coach. Burrow had been voted the Most Outstanding Defensive Player on the freshman team. The coach says, 'I'm not going to be the first coach to give a walk-on a scholarship.'

"That's the point I'm trying to make. Think about that: in 1970 the University of Mississippi refused to give Jimmy Burrow a scholarship because the head coach did not want to be the first coach to ever give a walk-on a scholarship. *What does he do?* I said, 'I'll give him one.' It just happened Coach Devaney has a meeting. We've got three quarterbacks, no scout-team quarterbacks. We got freshmen and three upperclassmen. We bring Jimmy Burrow in as a scout-team quarterback because he had played quarterback in high school for me. When I left he was a sophomore. We knew he could do it. He was our scout team quarterback in 1971. In 1972 and '73, [he] makes all-conference free safety. That's what you get. My point being they wouldn't even give him a scholarship because he was a walk-on. Here we are at Nebraska, and we took 75 walk-ons a year. You'd think:

any marginal kid, 50–50, 60–40 guy that we didn't recruit still wanted to come here and prove they could play. That's what permeated the whole state. That's why we got them all."

Osborne said the key to Nebraska's walk-on program was integrity and equal opportunity.

Treating all players equally fostered an environment where walk-ons wanted to play at Nebraska. The Huskers also took full advantage of the rules at that time, allowing them to field the biggest roster in college football. "When Bob Devaney came here, each conference had its own regulations as to squad size. In the Big 8, we had 45 initials. You could bring in 45 new guys, and there was no upper limit," Osborne said. "If you kept them all eligible, you could have 160 guys on scholarship. Then the first year that I became the head coach—in '73—the NCAA decided we're not going to have individual conference regulations. We're going to go to a national standard. At that time I think they kind of ratcheted it down, but it seemed like they might have said the initial number would be like 30, and the total number would be maybe 110. They gave you an upper number. I remember in the Southwest Conference they could bring in 50 initials, but they had an overall cap of 100. There was a book called *Meat on the Hoof* that was written about University of Texas because all the schools down there were bringing in 50 players and then they had to get down to 100 because if you bring in 50 each year, you're going to be at 200. I think Texas—and I'm sure other places—they had these drills where they were designed to run guys off. They were really pretty brutal. That's how they got down to the total of 100. We had no upper limit and we had a freshman team.

"Then when we went to the reduced numbers and eventually that got down to the current 85 total and 25 initials, I began to notice that sometimes the best players we had were not the first five or 10 that we offered scholarships to. We only had 45. It might be the 42nd or the 43rd or the 45th. I think Tony Davis was one of the last players we offered out of Tecumseh and probably would have been 44th or 45th, and he was our best running back. When they cut down the numbers, I thought if we get players to walk on, I'm sure there are players here in the state of Nebraska who would have qualified for a scholarship if we'd had 45. Now we're down to 30 or 25 or whatever it was. I thought, *If we can get a fair number of those guys to come as walk-ons, it would give us the same effect because a certain percentage of those guys are going to turn out to be really good players.* The other thing that was to our advantage was that we didn't have a Nebraska State. We had the University of Nebraska and certainly at that time we had Nebraska-Kearney or Nebraska-Omaha, but a lot of players would be willing to walk on here. We got a pretty high-level walk-on player.

"The other thing that we did was that we made sure it was an absolute meritocracy. If a player came in and he was better than some walk-on scholarship guy, we gave him a scholarship. When we were down to 25 initials, we never gave out 25 initials. We give out 20, 21, maybe 22, but we'd always saved three or four every year for walk-ons. We told players: 'If you come in at the end of spring ball and you're first or second at your position, then we're going to give you a scholarship. First or second in your position going into the fall camp after your first year or second year or whenever, if you can rise to the depth chart one or two, then you're going to be on scholarship.' That's what we did. I think there were places where they did have walk-ons, but a lot of times they were treated differently. I remember LSU had a practice field that was quite a ways away, and scholarship players would get on the bus. They bussed them down to the practice field, and the walk-ons had to walk down, and they were treated like subhuman individuals. I think most of the players on our team, they really couldn't have named who was a scholarship player and who was a walk-on. Unless they roomed with them or something, there was no distinction in the way they were treated, and [we] were able to give them access to the training table and also to the study hall. That made a big difference."

The other thing about the walk-on program at Nebraska that didn't show up on any stat sheet was the connection those players brought to the locker room and the entire state. Every community felt like they owned a piece of Nebraska football when they had a player on the team. Often, it was those players who welcomed out-of-state scholarship players to their homes during breaks and holidays.

A group of guys from the West Coast might spend the weekend in a small Nebraska community hunting or fishing with teammates. It wasn't uncommon to see a walk-on player host large groups at family cabins over the Fourth of July to jet ski or go boating. They not only brought a Nebraska work ethic to the program, but they also added a family feel to welcome out-of-state players. "Think about the average walk-on in Nebraska," former assistant coach Ron Brown said. "Think about where these kids came from—ranchers and farmers and kids that came from small towns and so forth, kids that not a lot of people had noticed them nationally. They were eight-man football players, six-man football players. It's everything against all of the new exciting and flash-in-the-pan stuff out there. Tom resonated with that. He made that such a priority that those kids not only could be a part of our program but be leaders in a program that would earn scholarships...They set the tone for effort and training and doing extra things and doing a great job academically and being the very best that you could be in every area of your life. They were the guys that came from off these farms and ranches. They were the ones setting the tone. Not only were they just kind of, 'Well, let's see if we can find a place for a walk-on kid.' It wasn't like that. It was more like, 'Man, this kid will bring something to the table that'll help lead our football team.' He may earn a scholarship and become a great player like a lot of them did, but they'll also lead in ways, maybe even quietly, lead in ways of what work ethic and physicality and playing circumstance free, no matter how bad the weather is. They set the tone for these kids who came from warm weather climates and maybe had a little bit more flash in the pan where we needed that grit to be the football team that would win national championships. We needed those guys."

PART 4

THE PLAYERS

14

Rex Burkhead

ON PAPER THERE WAS NOTHING THAT NECESSARILY JUMPED out about Rex Burkhead. Growing up in suburban Dallas, he was a 5'10", 190-pound white running back. Anyone, however, who spent time around Burkhead quickly learned why he took on the nickname of "Superman" in high school.

Burkhead was special in every which way. Not only was he one of the top football players in Texas coming out of high school, but he also ended his time at Nebraska as one of the most respected and beloved Huskers in recent history. By the end of Burkhead's career, young boys all over the state wore his No. 22 jersey. His story is so much more than football. He's the definition of the type of player every coach dreams about having in their program.

While recruiting Burkhead, former NU assistant coach Marvin Sanders watched tape of him with Bo Pelini. "Bo's big thing was when he turns on the film: is he a good football player?

I remember watching the film as a staff on Rex Burkhead, and you knew right then this guy is just a good football player," Sanders said. "I don't care what his size is, what his color is—not that that would ever matter. We didn't ask what his 40 was. I couldn't tell you to this day what we thought his 40 was. We knew when we threw him on that football field that this guy is a good football player."

Burkhead was more than good. He played varsity football at the 6A level in Texas as a freshman. Plano High School had an enrollment of nearly 5,000 students. Burkhead stood out so much that he was on the varsity despite not even being in the senior high building, which houses only 11th and 12th graders. "Rex was just a different breed," former teammate and class of 2009 Nebraska recruit C.J. Zimmerer said. "He was one of the few guys that even as a freshman in college he was so detailed about what he was eating. His stretching routine, his body care routine, it was just next level compared to the rest of us. I was a scout teamer. The nutrition stuff wasn't as important to me, and I didn't understand. A lot of us didn't understand why Rex was so into that stuff. This is the reason why. It just extends your career, extends your body's ability to do things. He's so smart, too—academically and football-wise, just a great all-around dude, and a great athlete. I've seen him play basketball. He can pick up any type of ball. He could probably hop on a skateboard. He would be great at anything he does. I know he is a great person, a great dad to a couple of kiddos, and all those things just extend your life in a place like the NFL."

When Burkhead was on campus for a recruiting visit in the summer of 2008, Supreme Court Justice Clarence Thomas was also in Lincoln, Nebraska. Thomas is a huge Huskers fan and immediately knew who Burkhead was. That's the type of impact Burkhead had. His talents even caught the eye of a United States

Supreme Court Justice. "He was recruited out of Plano, and I ran into his mother and I was just standing around," Thomas said in 2013. "Rex was there on his recruiting trip, and his mother was there, and they let me into the locker room like one of the guys. His mother was standing in that hall outside, and we were recruiting [linebacker] Phillip Dillard's brother [Gabe Lynn], and I was talking to his mother. Then Rex's mother said, 'I'm a recruit's mother, too.' She mentioned to me who he was, and I was like, 'Oh yeah, he's a four-star, Superman.'"

Burkhead's Nebraska coaches raved about him on and off the field. "Rex was just the ultimate, all-around tremendous person and player," former Nebraska special teams and defensive coordinator John Papuchis said. "[He] had a big heart, cared for his teammates, cared for the community, loved being part of the Nebraska family and community but was such a good football player. He was as good of a pound-for-pound player as I've ever been around on a daily basis. If you could say, 'Okay, what's a coach's dream?' He is it. He does everything that he is ever asked to do. He does it to the best of his ability and he represents the program in a 100 percent first-class way in every way that he could off the field."

Said defensive line coach Rick Kaczenski: "He's the type of guy you hope your daughter marries. When I think about Rex, you're like, 'Man, I wish I could be that good of a person.' Look at him in the NFL. One, he's dependable, he's tough, he's smart. You know exactly what the hell you're getting. Rex, he's a coach for those younger guys. I remember him talking to me or talking to these young backs. He knew the guys we were recruiting. He knew the running backs. We were, 'Hey, we are recruiting a kid from Katy [Texas].'

"'Yes, man. Hey, he's good.' Just that. He wanted Nebraska to be successful after Rex Burkhead had left. Nebraska meant more than just the time he spent there. By any stretch of the imagination, I'm not going to say I'm close with Rex, but as an outside observer, Rex is one of the best human beings I've ever had the privilege of being around in my life, just an unbelievable kid."

* * *

If not for a knee injury that caused Burkhead to miss six full games as a senior in 2012, he was well on his way to becoming a 4,000-yard rusher at Nebraska. The only two backs that can say that are former Heisman Trophy winner Mike Rozier and Ameer Abdullah.

Burkhead's 2012 injury helped Abdullah's career take off at NU. Burkhead finished with 3,329 yards rushing, while Abdullah had 4,588 after his career ended in 2014. But Burkhead remained very supportive of Abdullah. "Ameer Abdullah comes in and takes your place, and you're supposed to be the Heisman candidate for that year," former NU assistant coach Ron Brown said. "Here you are now in your senior year and now you've had a stellar junior year.

"You led the conference in rushing...Now here comes young gun Ameer Abdullah running for over 1,000 yards and having a great year while you played half the games because of that knee injury that you sustained in the first game of the year. He could have gone in the tank and quit. You know what he did? He came to every meeting, he was in here for all the stuff, he was at every practice, and he's pouring his guts out in this kid, and he's fighting to get back on that field. He does. He finished his career. I'll never forget that Georgia game we lost down there in the Capital One Bowl. What a great game he had against a team that was a play away from playing for the national title.

He's a sixth-round draft pick. I knew Marvin Lewis from the old days. Marvin drafted him in the sixth round with the Cincinnati Bengals, and I knew Marvin was getting something special, but it never stops with him."

Brown knew there was something different about Burkhead. So he's not surprised that he's gone on to have one of the longest pro careers of any Nebraska running back in history. "I told those pro people this is the guy you want on your team," Brown said. "For all the ups and downs that people think about him, Bill Belichick knows what he needs on a championship football team. He had the right guy when he got Burkhead and he's a consummate pro."

During the Huskers' inaugural season in the Big Ten in 2011, Burkhead was third in the league in rushing with 1,357 yards on 284 carries for 15 touchdowns. He was a unanimous first-team All-Big Ten selection. During the first ever Heroes Trophy game against Iowa, Burkhead carried the ball 38 times for 160 yards. There wasn't anything flashy about the performance. It was just tough November Big Ten football.

The most interesting part, though, was Burkhead wanted no part of breaking Cory Ross' mark set in the 2003 Alamo Bowl against Michigan State. Ross had carried the ball 37 times in Bo Pelini's first ever win as a head coach. "I said, 'Rex, look at the crowd here. We're going to have to hand you the ball probably 30-something times," Brown recalled of the 2011 Iowa game. "Bo was breathing down my back because [Burkhead] told me, 'Coach, I don't want to get carries where I'm just kneeling down and just so I can break the record.' It was the record of number of carries in the game, and Bo wanted him to have that. Bo and I were at it.

"I said, 'Come on, Bo. He doesn't really want it that way, man. That's all right. Another day, another time.'

"He's like, 'No, I wanted it.' I got him in there. Rex reluctantly went in, took a knee. I felt bad for the kid, but that's just who he is. He's a very humble guy. I just loved his attitude. He was an academic All-American twice. He's a great example of Nebraska football. I don't know, maybe it sure seemed the crowd believed it because I'm not sure anybody ever got as loud of cheers when they introduced the starting lineup from the big screen that Rex did."

The most meaningful thing Burkhead did during his time at Nebraska led to one of the best moments we've seen with Nebraska football in years. When Burkhead was injured in 2012, he received a letter from a young seven-year-old boy and his family. That boy was Jack Hoffman from Atkinson, Nebraska. Hoffman was diagnosed with pediatric brain cancer. Jack's father, Andy, reached out to Burkhead to see if he'd meet with his son and offer support as he was about to undergo several extensive surgeries and treatments.

Burkhead took things to a whole another level. He started wearing a Team Jack bracelet to show support for the small grassroots campaign Hoffman and his family began in 2012. The next thing you know, several Huskers football players began wearing bracelets and T-shirts to support Hoffman. During the 2012 Wisconsin game, Burkhead and Hoffman helped lead the Huskers out during the Tunnel Walk. It's one of the only times in the history of the Tunnel Walk that somebody besides a Huskers player helped lead the team out. The other was in 2001 when a group of first responders led NU out after the terrorist attacks on 9/11. "The original thing was just our team relationship with Team Jack, and Rex passed out bracelets," said C.J. Zimmerer, Burkhead's former NU teammate. "People started wearing those around and then we were approached by a nonprofit called Uplifting Athletes, which was established by Scott Shirley up at Penn State when he was a player. The goal was to promote a rare disease through football and try to raise money."

Team Jack quickly became a household name around Huskers Nation. In addition to the players themselves, Nebraska fans started buying T-shirts and bracelets to show their support for Hoffman. Local shops began carrying Team Jack merchandise, too. "Do you want to know why Rex Burkhead was a great player? Watch him when he wasn't playing. What did he do? He teams up with this kid, this young boy named Jack," Brown said. "He's got cancer, and [Burkhead] starts a national fundraiser for this kid. He wins a national award for a guy who had the greatest impact on diseases and so forth of anybody in college football. That's who Rex Burkhead is."

Burkhead and Zimmerer would also help start a road race to fundraise for Team Jack. (In 2025 the race completed its 13th year, and well over $125,000 had been raised for Team Jack and pediatric brain cancer.) All of these efforts from Burkhead set up *the* moment in 2013. Bo Pelini wanted to do something for Hoffman and his family during the spring game. He and director of operations Jeff Jamrog came up with a plan to put Hoffman into the spring game for one play. They designed a touchdown run that would go viral, but nobody had any idea a moment like this was about to be delivered. "Bo got on the headset and he goes, 'Joe, drop a player and get Jack in," said former graduate assistant and Husker quarterback Joe Ganz. "I was like, 'Huh? What are you talking about?'

"He goes, 'Let Jack run the touchdown.'

"I was like, 'All right. Does everybody else know?'

"He's like, 'Yes, don't worry about it. Draw a play.'

"There's a picture of me, him, and [quarterback] Taylor [Martinez]. I'm just drawing a play on the sideline and say, 'Hey, you're going to get the ball.' I didn't do a great job because Jack went the wrong way to start. That's a coaching error. I drew it up. I was like, 'Hey, we're going to hand you the ball off, and you're going to run this way.' I can't remember how old he was at the time, maybe seven, eight.

"He just looked at me, 'Okay.'

"I was like, 'This is going to be awesome.' Then it happened. You knew in the moment. You're like, 'Holy shit.' That was something that is pretty special because it was in the middle of the spring game…Then you see him out there and hand the ball off. Then everybody ran. I was like, 'Holy cow. That was pretty cool.'"

The play would go on to win the ESPY award for the Best Sports Moment of the Year in 2013. The video on Nebraska's official YouTube page received more than 9 million views. All of this raised more awareness for Team Jack and their efforts to raise money for pediatric brain cancer. The organization has generated well over $9 million for pediatric brain cancer since it started in 2013, and Burkhead's support for the Hoffman family was a major reason why.

Sadly, Jack's father, Andy, died from Glioblastoma, an aggressive brain cancer, in 2021. He was 42 years old. Jack sadly died as well on January 15, 2025, losing his 14-year battle with cancer. Burkhead remained by his side the entire time, including at his funeral services in Atkinson. Zimmerer reflected on Jack's run. "Just with social media and everything, it's hard to keep a secret these days. Nobody knew about it really except the team, which was great, and that I think brought on the emotions out of the stadium where people are getting choked up right away."

Zimmerer stood right next to Hoffman after Martinez handed him the football. "In my five years at Nebraska, that's definitely my best memory without a doubt—most impactful for sure and very proud that I got to be a part of it."

15

Zac Taylor

Before quarterback Zac Taylor came to Nebraska in 2005, everything about him said he was an Oklahoma Sooner. He grew up in Norman, Oklahoma, and attended Norman High, where he shined at quarterback, throwing for 1,950 yards and 16 touchdowns as a senior. His father, Sherwood, was a captain for Barry Switzer's 1979 Oklahoma team that finished 11–1 and won the Orange Bowl against Florida State. Sherwood's teams posted a 32–3 record during his three-year career at OU. His mother, Julie, also attended Oklahoma and was a die-hard Sooners fan. The Taylor family would later have season tickets to OU games. They were next-door neighbors with Gary Gibbs, who succeeded Switzer as head coach after the Sooners were placed on NCAA probation. Even Zac's sister, Kathryn, who also stars as a Special Olympic swimmer, worked in the OU Dining Hall, serving Oklahoma student-athletes daily.

By the time Taylor's senior season rolled around in the fall of 2001, Oklahoma was on top of the college football mountain. In 2000 Bob Stoops captured the national championship in his second season as head coach. Taylor, though, was nowhere near OU's radar. In 2002 the Sooners signed four-star athlete/quarterback Paul Thompson and four-star quarterback Noah Allen out of Texas. "My junior year is really when I started being recruited. I knew nothing about the process. I wasn't even a starter as a sophomore," Taylor said. "My junior year I had a good season…really, my first year as a starter, I had a great year. I didn't know how the scholarship thing worked. I had no scholarships. Oklahoma then wins the national championship in January. Fast forward to April, I got my first offers from Colorado, Wake Forest, and Oklahoma State. Then I'm going to the summer camps, and OU just won the national championship. I'm not even thinking that they're going to offer me a scholarship. I'm getting offers from teams that went 3–8 last year. [Oklahoma QB coach and former Iowa quarterback] Chuck Long was a really good friend of my dad. He lived in town, got to know my dad pretty well, and so they wanted me to come to the camp. I went to the camp. He spent a lot of time with me, but I never got the impression that they were going to offer me, never expected it. There may have been something vague about walking on."

Taylor's primary recruiting attention initially came from Colorado, and in the summer of 2001, he was fully ready to commit to Gary Barnett and the Buffaloes. "I take an unofficial visit up there," Taylor said. "When I got there, they saw a 6'1", 155-pound stick figure and realized: this kid is pretty small, pretty skinny. When I got back to Norman, they pulled my offer."

Taylor was left scrambling, but then brand-new Oklahoma State head coach Les Miles and his offensive coordinator Mike Gundy got involved. Colorado pulled their offer, Oklahoma wasn't an option, and then the Sooners' in-state rival looked like a viable landing spot for Taylor.

"I panicked and I commit to Oklahoma State because I now see that offers could be pulled, and it makes me nervous," Taylor said. "On the 4th of July, I commit to Oklahoma State and then go through the whole year. Josh Fields—I don't know if you remember that name—he was a true freshman quarterback at Oklahoma State and he goes in and beats Oklahoma. He's a year ahead of me, hosts me during my visit at Oklahoma State. He's the big celebrity on campus. I'm like: this doesn't really make sense for me."

That's when Wake Forest became Taylor's last hope. Jim Grobe had just been hired in Winston-Salem, North Carolina. His linebackers coach, Brad Lambert, played for Sherwood Taylor at Kansas State when he served as an assistant for Jim Dickey. That connection to Lambert gave Taylor an opportunity at Wake Forest, and that's how he ended up with the Demon Deacons. It was a recruiting class that would later help Wake Forest capture an ACC championship in 2006. However, Taylor quickly realized he made a mistake once he arrived in Winston-Salem. Yes, he had a seat at a table, but he knew very little about his new school. "I didn't really do my homework when I committed out there. Again, I just knew I didn't want to go to Oklahoma State," Taylor said. "The only offer I had left was Wake, and I took a visit over winter break. I don't even know if that was legal at the time, to be honest with you. There were no kids on campus. It was cold. It was a pretty campus. I thought, *Let's do it. I'll go to Wake Forest.*

"When I get there, I realized it was a lot more zone-read-type stuff than I was prepared for. They had other quarterbacks on the roster that were way better at it than I was—way better fits for the system. I hadn't really matured physically yet. I was like 180 pounds and didn't have a very strong arm. I wasn't fast, didn't really ever put myself in a position to be a player for them. I went through my first year, redshirted, went through my second year. I was the backup quarterback, only played a couple of snaps. Just at the end of the year, I wasn't happy there. There were 3,500 kids as undergrad students, which was the size of my high school. It was a very difficult academic school. Football there amongst the students wasn't a big deal. We were the No. 1 team in the country at basketball, Chris Paul, all those guys, just really wasn't a fit for me. I'd go home to Norman and I remember thinking like, *Man, I just want to go somewhere where football really matters like it does Norman.* You see all the Oklahoma bumper stickers, never thinking I'd be up at Nebraska. I remember it was probably November of my redshirt freshman year. I called my dad going to class and I said, 'I don't want to be here anymore. What are my options?'

"He said, 'We can get you to Southwest Missouri State or somewhere in Missouri, or I can go look at these junior colleges I used to recruit in Kansas.'

"I said, 'Why don't you do that?' He went to Coffeyville and Butler and just felt better about Butler and sent me to Butler. I never visited there or anything, but that's how I ended up."

Taylor's NCAA eligibility clock was ticking. He had already used up two seasons at Wake, including his redshirt. That meant he had little margin for error at Butler Community College in El Dorado, Kansas. He arrived at Butler in January of 2004. In a lot of ways, Taylor needed Butler. It was an opportunity for him to shine and get reps at a high level of junior college football, something he couldn't do at Wake Forest. "Butler was an unbelievable fit for me. Just the coaches that were there, the kids that were on the team, they reminded me way more of kids I grew up with in Norman, as opposed to being at Wake, where it was a bunch of kids that went to private schools in the Northeast," Taylor said. "I was way out of my element there. You know what I mean? I was friends with all the football players who came from the same background as I did, but just the students that went there—nothing against them—it just was a very different scene for me. Where I went to El Dorado, Kansas, I fit in way better. I've spent many hours on ranches at my grandparents' house out in the middle of nowhere. You go to El Dorado, and I felt way more at home, really enjoyed it. They'd won the national championship the year before I got there, just felt like I fit right in; I was really accepted. Coaches were excited to have me. There was an interesting mystique that comes with a player that transfers in from a Division I school. You're treated a little bit differently by the players there. They're in awe because that's where they want to get to, so they want to be friends with you, they want to ask you questions. *What was it like?* You immediately make friends that way because they're fascinated by what you've been through."

However, anyone who has watched *Last Chance U* on Netflix knows there are few guarantees at junior colleges. Often junior colleges oversign their roster by large amounts to ensure they have the best possible players in place. "They only keep 12 out-of-state players. That's the Jayhawk Conference rule. I did not know that. I also didn't know there was another quarterback there out of state that I was going to compete with," Taylor said. "It was a stressful spring. You're splitting reps with this kid from Colorado who's a good player. You realize quickly: once other kids are telling you how this all works, one of us is not going to be here by the end of the spring. I began asking myself the question if I made a mistake. It also coincided with the time that I was getting a lot bigger. I was about 200 pounds at that point. My arm had gotten stronger. I was in the system that gave me a lot of confidence. They didn't ask me to run or throw a lot of play-action. I was in the gun and a drop-back passer. That was way more in line with the type of player I saw myself as. I had an offensive coordinator named Aaron Flores, who has since passed away, but he was phenomenal at just getting you to be confident in yourself. He was a great playcaller. He did a good job utilizing the talent that we had and just puts you in unbelievable situations and was super aggressive. I still try to get my playcalling identity from him as he was aggressive at all times. I really, really enjoyed being there and being a part of that program."

* * *

Bill Callahan had just finished his first season at Nebraska in 2004. The Huskers went 5–6 and failed to qualify for a bowl game for the first time since 1968. Callahan was looking for a quarterback. He already had a commitment from national top 100 high school quarterback Harrison Beck. When they took his commitment, it canceled a June visit that was in the books for eventual USC quarterback Mark Sanchez.

NU was all in on Beck, but they quickly realized they needed another veteran quarterback in the class. The other quarterbacks on the 2004 roster were not ready to run Callahan's complicated West Coast Offense. Callahan was one year removed from coaching in the Super Bowl before taking the Nebraska job, and the 2004 season was a real struggle to get his offense off the ground. By sheer coincidence Zac Taylor watched Nebraska's offense firsthand in Norman, Oklahoma, on November 13, 2004. Butler was preparing for the NJCAA national championship game on November 28 in Coffeyville, Kansas, against Mississippi's Pearl River Community College and had the weekend off.

Taylor went home to Norman to watch the Sooners and Huskers square off in a night game. Little did Taylor know he would be quarterbacking the Huskers against Oklahoma in Lincoln, Nebraska, next season. "I was in junior college, not being recruited by Oklahoma at the time," Taylor said. "I probably had a Marshall and Memphis offer. During my bye week at Butler, I just went down to Norman, was visiting my parents, and they had tickets to the Nebraska game and I watched Jason White, I think, break some NCAA record. He completed like 23 straight passes. About a month later, I get an offer from Nebraska. A month after that, I'm on campus, and a month after that, I'm in the weight room. It was just a wild four months, when you look at me walking into a stadium as a junior college player with no offer from Nebraska or Oklahoma, no dog in a fight, just watching the game and then being in the weight room four or five months later."

It had been a long road for Taylor to get to this point. Callahan gave him the opportunity of a lifetime. Before the Huskers offered, he was probably heading to Marshall. Now a coach himself, Taylor laughed at what his mother Julie asked Callahan during his recruiting visit to Nebraska. "My mom was in Bill Callahan's office with me on my recruiting visit, and we're talking, and he's selling us on the program, and she just cuts through it. She's like, 'Tell me he's going to start.'

"I said, 'Mom, stop. It doesn't work like that.'

"She's like, 'He only has got two years left. I just want to make sure. I'm worried,'" Taylor said.

"Bill laughed it off and gave the coachspeak around it: 'We're going to play the best players, but he's going to have a great opportunity to earn the job.' Of course, it was embarrassing for any kid when their mom speaks up like that, but those were our concerns, where there's a lot of competition there."

Taylor would go on to win the job at Nebraska that spring, beating out 2004 starter Joe Dailey, and Beck would not get to campus until June of 2005. The one real advantage Taylor had was his maturity. He was 22 years in June of 2005. When Beck arrived to campus, he was still 17 year, turning 18 in September. Operating Callahan's offense took a high level of discipline and maturity. Taylor had that and he also had toughness.

The signature moment when Taylor won over everybody was during a spring scrimmage in 2005. It was a week before the Red–White spring game. Callahan brought his team into Memorial Stadium. He took the green jerseys off his quarterbacks. It was a one vs. one scrimmage that lasted more than three hours and went 180-plus plays. Taylor had been sick with the flu that week but still strapped it on to scrimmage. He took eight sacks in that scrimmage but continued to keep getting up. He had blood coming off his lip. In addition to demonstrating his resilience, he quickly earned the respect of his teammates because that was the best the offense had looked under Callahan to date. "He came in. He just shut up. He worked his ass off. Honestly, what guys remember about him is he was one of the toughest dudes to ever take a snap under center," said Joe Ganz who was one of the Nebraska quarterbacks competing against Taylor that spring. "I know there was a ton of guys in the past like Scott Frost and all those guys that were renowned for how tough they were, right? I'd put Zac up there with any of those guys with how truly tough he was, and it was that spring scrimmage where it was the difference between you look at Zac

Taylor's career and then you look at Harrison Beck's career. It was that one scrimmage where coach made us all the quarterbacks live. Zac stood in there and took sacks."

The following year, in the spring of 2006, Callahan allowed Beck to earn his stripes in a similar type of scrimmage. Taylor was already locked in as the guy for 2006, but Beck got the same look. On a play where Beck was about to take a sack from eventual first-round draft pick defensive end Adam Carriker, he faked a hamstring injury to avoid getting hit. That was essentially the last of Beck at Nebraska. He left Lincoln during the middle of a two-a-day practice session in August of 2006 and never returned. Now he is best known for his TikTok posts under the handle @TheThrowGod. "[Taylor] had to get stitches in his lip, busted his lip, and then Harrison fake pulled a hamstring because Adam Carriker didn't bite on a naked play," Ganz said, comparing the two spring scrimmages. "I would put [Taylor] up there as one of the toughest quarterbacks to ever play here. To me, as a quarterback, that's probably one of the most important things is you aren't asked to do a whole lot of the game physically, right? You better be a tough dude in that pocket and stand in there and take shots for your team and deliver the football because of all the other shit that everybody else has to do."

Taylor got Nebraska as close to winning a conference championship as any player in the post-title era. In 2006 he led the Huskers to the Big 12 title game in Kansas City against his hometown Oklahoma Sooners. Taylor was named the Big 12 Offensive Player of the Year after throwing for 3,197 yards and 26 touchdowns. He finished his two-year career with 5,850 yards passing and 45 touchdowns. He also delivered a great come-from-behind win against Michigan in the 2005 Alamo Bowl. In 2017 he was inducted into the Nebraska Football Hall of Fame and he's the last NU offensive player to be named a conference player of the year.

The 2006 Huskers lost five games, but you can argue they easily could've beaten Texas, Oklahoma State, Oklahoma, and Auburn. That was a 9–5 team that felt more like it had a chance to be 12–2 or 13–1. "If you look at 2006, there were some games, man, where people just did not want to deal with us, the way we could run the ball and be efficient with the play action," Taylor said. "I don't think they ever got that No. 1 receiver they were looking for in the recruitment process. I know we were always close on a lot of guys that maybe went elsewhere, but they did a heck of a job finding linemen, finding big tight ends, and finding running backs. They had quarterbacks that were about to come through with all those guys like Blaine Gabbert and Josh Freeman and all those guys. It was really close, and unfortunately, just never really got a chance to get it all through. If I just have two better quarterback performances [against Oklahoma and Oklahoma State], you're looking at 11–2, and you beat Oklahoma, and you're playing in the Fiesta Bowl against Boise State, and then you got a chance to have 2006 up there in the rafters and you won the conference title there. Really, it's as close as you could possibly get to being regarded as a really great team. I thought we had great players that had tremendous college careers. From top to bottom, our roster was really good. Special teams was great. We took a lot of pride in special teams. Those guys blocking kicks and just really thought it was a fantastic team from top to bottom, that was just a couple of games away from being one of those top teams in recent history."

When Taylor's time at Nebraska was over, he quickly learned he was not built for the NFL and he had very little interest in playing football in Canada after a short stint in Winnipeg.

Taylor had just recently married Sarah Sherman, the daughter of former Green Bay Packers head coach Mike Sherman. The two met while she was working as a graduate student in Nebraska's media relations office. Mike Sherman was named Texas A&M's head coach in November of 2007 shortly after Callahan was fired at Nebraska. With nothing else on the table, Taylor chose to take a graduate assistant job in College Station, Texas, under his new father-in-law. The other connection he had to Sherman was Tim Cassidy, Nebraska's former director of operations. He was now in the same role under Sherman at Texas A&M.

Taylor was the low man on the totem pole. He served as a graduate assistant under Sherman for four seasons. "I worked for my father-in-law, and he was going to make certain that people didn't think I had the easy way into the job," Taylor said, laughing. "I was there all night till 2:00 AM, drawing pass pictures and getting them all wrong in the presentations. He's ripping my butt. It was hard. My first year, I wasn't even on the field. I was quality control. I wasn't even the GA, so I didn't get to coach on the field like I thought I deserved to because I had a huge ego because I just got done playing quarterback in Nebraska and I thought I had all the answers. Coaching's got a way of humbling you. This profession does, and so I spent four years there really building myself up and didn't realize how much I had to learn in the game of football. I was fortunate to be around some of the best teachers imaginable at A&M on that offensive staff. I learned a lot at Texas A&M in these four years. It was a grind. We started at the bottom. We were a terrible team our first year. By that third year, we're at the Cotton Bowl with the share of the Big 12 South, so we saw the highs and lows of college football at its finest there."

Another funny twist to Taylor's early coaching career is he worked with his wife, Sarah, at Texas A&M. "She was Tim Cassidy's recruiting assistant," Taylor said. "My first year of marriage was 2009, and I'm there in 2008. I'm a GA. I'm not good at it. I'm really bad at all the drawing pictures and breaking down tape. I'm bad. I'm just out of college, I don't know what I'm doing, so my father-in-law's coming to my office, ripping me, and I'm getting yelled at. It's my first year of marriage, which isn't always perfect, so maybe I got into a fight with my wife the night before and so I can't go that direction in the hallway because that's her desk. I can't go the other direction because it's my father-in-law. He's yelling at me. It was a lot those first couple of years, but it was fun looking back on it. I wouldn't change it for anything. We all grew up the right way, doing it the hard way."

He didn't get his first full-time assistant coaching job until 2012 in the NFL with the Miami Dolphins when Sherman became their offensive coordinator. Taylor was with the Dolphins from 2012 to 2015 and then spent one season back in college football under Tommy Tuberville at Cincinnati in 2016. The staff was fired following that season, but then Taylor's big coaching break came in 2017 when he got an opportunity under Sean McVay with the Los Angeles Rams. In 2018 they played for the Super Bowl, and Taylor's stock soared. He interviewed for multiple NFL head coaching jobs and landed with the Cincinnati Bengals. In 2020 they drafted Joe Burrow, the 2019 Heisman Trophy-winning quarterback from LSU whose father played at Nebraska. In 2021 the Bengals played in the Super Bowl against the Rams and McVay, one of Taylor's mentors. Taylor found his calling in the NFL and he's gone on to have one of the most successful coaching careers of a former Husker.

Even though Taylor is knee-deep in NFL life, he still closely follows Nebraska. In 2022 he spoke to the Huskers' women's basketball team before a Big Ten tournament game in Indianapolis. In 2022 he also was on the sideline for Nebraska's game at Michigan. In 2021 Taylor's oldest son, Brooks, even wore a Nebraska jersey and hat in Norman to cheer on the Huskers against the Sooners while sitting with Sherwood and Julie and being surrounded by OU fans. "I look back fondly on interacting with all the great people there in Nebraska," Taylor said. "So many of them are still there in some capacity in the athletic department or academics or even the cafeteria. The biggest regret I had was being there only a brief time, never getting a chance to go through the state and go see all the people that watch games in the local coffee shop in western Nebraska and out on the farms doing all their work, and they just look forward to those games on Saturday. There's not a day that I don't meet a Nebraska fan in an airport or somewhere, or a friend of mine says, 'Hey, I got a relative that is the biggest Nebraska fan ever.' That's how you would define every Nebraska fan. They're all the biggest Nebraska fans ever. That's so unique. You don't get that everywhere, and it's what really makes Nebraska so special."

16

Sam Foltz

THE LATE SAM FOLTZ MIGHT BE ONE OF THE BEST FOUR-SPORT high school athletes to come out of Nebraska in years. However, it wasn't his athletic ability he's remembered for. Foltz had a unique gift to make every person he interacted with feel important. He was special, and that's why so many people still remember his legacy to this day. Foltz's life was taken in a tragic car accident in Merton, Wisconsin, on July 23, 2016. Also lost in the accident was Michigan State punter Mike Sadler. Before that dark day in July, Foltz was set to have a long career in the NFL after his senior season in 2016. In 2015 he was the Big Ten's punter of the year.

His journey to become one of the best punters in the sport was unorthodox. Foltz grew up in the small Nebraska town of Greeley, about 50 miles north of Grand Island. His older brother, Jordan, attended high school in Greeley, while Sam and his sisters, Caroline and Betsy, went to Class A Grand Island for more opportunities. Foltz's family lived on a farm in Greeley and owned a home in Grand Island. Gerald Foltz operated the family farm, while his wife, Jill Foltz, served as the school nurse at Grand Island Senior High School. The family would go back and forth between the two communities in Greeley and Grand Island.

It became apparent right away that Sam Foltz was a special athletic talent. As a senior in 2011, he was All-Nebraska as a defensive back with 84 tackles and four interceptions. He also led the Islanders with 39 catches for 686 yards and 10 touchdowns. He punted for Grand Island as well, but nobody could've predicted that was his future path. At that time he was more of a great athlete that punted. In track he ran the 400-meter dash in 49.01 seconds, was a standout American Legion baseball player in the summer, and played basketball in the winter. Everything Foltz touched turned to gold. However, he was so busy with his commitment to being a four-sport athlete that he didn't spend much time attending camps and recruiting events for football. His baseball team in the summer had a very strict policy about missing games to participate in summer football camps.

Before his senior season, Foltz and his family came across Kohl's Kicking Camps. These events feature the premier kickers and punters in the country from high school to the NFL. At the Division I football level, Foltz thought he could play both safety and wide receiver, but he knew punting might also be his ticket. It was his first ever kicking camp he attended and, by accident, he signed up for the national elite prospect event. "I remember him from our national camp when he was going to be senior in high school," Jamie Kohl, the owner/founder of Kohl's Kicking Camps, said. "Jill accidentally signed him up for the National Scholarship Camp, which is the most competitive camp we have. I think they thought it was just a regular training camp because we run 100 events. Let's say we run 100 events a year, and 95 percent of them are training-based. [For the] 20 kids: get your film broke down, we're going to do drills, we're going to do different types of activities with the classroom, taking notes, and trying to help you become a better player so that you have tools you can work with. They signed up for the most cutthroat. We're going to compete, we're going to chart only the top guys—advance type stuff. Sam did really, really, really well. I remember thinking, *Man, this kid, who is still on a national level, was really, really talented and he's going to be a good one.* Then I remember leaving that camp feeling that him and Devon Bell, who played at Mississippi State and had a couple of tryouts with some other NFL teams, were two of the guys that were able to hit over five-second hang times at the high school level, which was tremendous. I just remember watching them punt, and those two are different. You could see that Sam, if he worked at it, was going to be really, really good."

Before Foltz eventually decided to walk on at Nebraska in 2012, he contemplated taking scholarship offers from a handful of Dakota schools at the Football Championship Series (FCS) level. They were all interested in him as a defensive back or wide receiver. Nobody knew they had a future NFL-caliber punter on their hands, as he was regarded as a high-level athlete. Bo Pelini's Nebraska staff made a strong push in the class of 2012 to bring in an elite group of walk-ons. In that class were future NFL players like fullback Andy Janovich and wide receiver Brandon Reilly. Several other eventual contributors like defensive end Ross Dzuris, tight end Trey Foster, quarterback Ryker Fyfe, kicker Spencer Lindsay, linebacker Brad Simpson, offensive lineman Dylan Utter, and running backs Graham Nabity and Jordan Nelson were a part of that 2012 walk-on class.

Foltz would also decide to join, making it one of the best modern-day Nebraska walk-on classes in history. "I was a part of that, and Coach Jamrog was a part of that, and we recruited the heck out of those guys," former assistant coach and in-state recruiter Barney Cotton said. "They all got home visits and official visits and everything like a scholarship guy. One of the guys I remember most—and it's unfortunate that he's not with us now—is Sam Foltz. Gerald, his dad, who I'm still good friends with, we're out eating at Wilderness Ridge out there on an official visit, and he was all set. He was going to one of the Dakota schools. He was going to take a full ride up there. After that official weekend in Lincoln, Gerald and I, we were just talking about it the other day. He said, 'I'm not going up north. I'm going to Nebraska.' He'd still be playing in a long NFL career had it not been the tragic accident that he had."

Another future contributor who would eventually join that walk-on class was offensive lineman Sam Hahn. The DeWitt Tri County product initially signed with North Dakota State and played his freshman year there in 2012, winning a national championship ring. He transferred to NU in January 2013. Hahn played in the 2012 Nebraska Shrine Bowl with Foltz and the other walk-ons who all chose to come to Lincoln. When Hahn and Foltz saw each other for the first time in Lincoln, they immediately hit it off, and the two became close friends because of their similar farming backgrounds.

Both were studying agronomy and would go on to have many of the same classes together on UNL's East Campus, which housed the agriculture majors. "I just asked him one time in class, 'What are you doing here? Aren't you from Grand Island?' He's like, 'Yes, I went to high school in Grand Island, but I'm actually from Greeley, and my family farms and stuff.' From that point on it was pretty much history," Hahn said of his friendship with Foltz. "I mean, we each had this farming background and from small towns and had the same major and things like that. Then, in that class, we helped each other out a little bit, asked each other questions, just going back and forth. I think that was the only class we were in together that semester. That would've been the spring semester of our freshman year in 2013. Then the next year, our sophomore year, we had a class or two together each semester. Then by the time we got to our junior and senior years, we pretty much just lined our schedules to take every class together just because we're the same major and we had to tweak stuff around a little bit because obviously our gen eds and things like that didn't line up from the beginning, but we pretty much took our whole core agronomy classes together and went through school together. That was good. We did a lot of studying together and things like that. That's how our relationship really was forged."

When Hahn first met Foltz, he wasn't a punter yet. In 2012 Foltz redshirted. Future NFL kicker Brett Maher punted and was the placekicker for the Big Red. He handled both duties in 2011 as well. All-American Alex Henery handled both duties before Maher. The Huskers had a hole in 2013. They didn't really have a true punter on the roster after being blessed with two NFL legs since 2007. Foltz played wide receiver in 2012, but the staff was aware of his punting talent. They gave him a shot at the job in the spring of 2013, and he beat out scholarship kicker Mauro Bondi, who primarily was a kickoff specialist. "He was transitioned to be a punter. He was still doing a little bit of both," Hahn said. "During spring ball it became evident that, I think, this is going to be our guy. He was still doing some—well, because I think they didn't know if he was going to be a safety or a DB or a receiver—then I think they looked at it and said, 'This kid's got both of them,' and he did some stuff that spring. And then going into fall camp, I'm pretty sure they just told him, 'Hey, we know you're really gifted and we're probably wasting some athleticism here, but you're going to be our punter,' because we had a pretty solid wide receiver room at that time. There was a good group, and you had some DBs that were doing well, and we need a punter."

Foltz didn't flinch. He jumped on the opportunity. Moving to punter gave him an opportunity to be a possible four-year starter at Nebraska. It also was the first time in Foltz's athletic career he could focus on one thing. He was no longer a four-sport athlete or a guy trying to figure out if he was a wide receiver or a safety. He was now a punter. Foltz could focus his elite athletic ability on mastering his new craft.

By July of 2013, he was back on the radar of Kohl. That offseason Kohl helped place Pat Smith from Western Illinois to Nebraska to be the Huskers' starting kicker in 2013. Smith replaced Maher at placekicker, while Foltz would punt. Foltz also served as the holder. Smith was heavily involved in Kohl's kicking events, and Foltz hopped in his car with him and headed out to the college showcase event in July of 2013. He was all in on his new position. Foltz would spend the next four summers at these events working with Kohl and the other top specialists in college football. In the summer of 2013, he had been the low man on the totem pole, but by 2016 he would be one of the faces of the event. "Pat Smith ends up going to Nebraska and he became friends with Sam, and he had Sam come to our college camp then the next summer because Sam was really young. So we gave Sam a duty of basically being an intern," Kohl said. "We called them a runner, basically running around collecting charts and—being for lack of a better term—'a grunt' for the other counselors that we had that were in charge of stations, that were in charge of making sure that the camp was running properly. Like I said, I didn't even have a station assigned to Sam, and by the end of that first weekend, it's a two or three-day camp. It would start on a Friday night and then it went through Sunday.

"By the end of that weekend, Sam had been someone that not only did I grow to like, I grew to really just say, 'This is a kid I really want to have around a bunch because of the humble work ethic, attitude, get-shit-done type guy he was.' You'd have to only tell him a thing once, and it was going to be done, and he had a way of commanding with his presence where the other coaches, even though some of them were four or five or 10 years older, they understood that Sam was someone that was serious about getting the job done, getting it done right. He wanted to perform in a way that people respected. To me, if you have those attributes in a nominal setting like that, that was going to carry over, and he was going to take that to the weight room, he was going to take that to the practice field, he was going to take that to the classroom. He was going to take that everywhere he went in life because in ways of looking at it, when I watch people and they don't know that I'm watching them, and I see them and I see them interact and I see how they perform, and when they check a bunch of those boxes, that's someone that's outstanding. Sam, in my mind, started solidifying that that summer. Then we go through the next year, and Sam continued to mature.

"All of a sudden now, he's starting to have success on the field and really growing to be someone. He had come to a couple of our events. I think he helped out in the Omaha camp with me. He came back to the league camp, came back, helped out at the scholarship camp, and really had been someone that, again, we enjoyed being around. He started having a lot of success. I think I came to a game and watched him in Lincoln and just was becoming a strong part of what we tried to do and really hopefully a guy that we could promote for the NFL. It was a win-win situation. Then the next summer, he signed up, I think it was a 10-day tour with my second-in-command coach, Luke Radke.

"Those guys traveled all over the country, and, I think, for Sam it was a cool opportunity. He wanted to get out of the Midwest a little bit. I think they started in Atlanta, and then they drove up the coast up to New York. Sam would help out with camp and then he would demonstrate every day when we'd go city to city. There'd be NFL guys, there'd be top college guys basically every day for 10 days straight. He was able to compete against really good players from all over the country on that road trip and coach high school kids, refining his craft as a punter, and helping him become a more detailed master of his profession. That was a really, really cool experience. I know him and Luke, they listened to country music, and they drove around. Sam was an enjoyable guy to be around from our perspective because we're in our 30s or 40s. You start losing touch a little bit with some of the 21, 22, 23-year-olds. In my way I think Sam was a little bit of an old soul. He was someone who could talk to anyone of any age and just put them at ease. Whether [it] was a young kid or a senior citizen, I always felt like Sam was someone who just could talk to people and make them feel comfortable where they were at in life.

"After that trip I had the opportunity then to work with Sam. We drove out to Omaha. We had a camp at Creighton Prep. He helped out for the day. I remember him pulling up in his big pickup truck, the one that Gerald [Foltz] still drives around, and just remarking at how he's transformed his body in just getting every inch of potential out of what he was capable of. Sam was someone—obviously, he was a very good athlete.

He was strong, one of the pound-for-pound strongest guys on the Huskers. We talked a lot about what he'd been doing in the weight room and how that was going to transfer over and how that was going to lead to just a really dynamic senior season, where in my opinion he was going to be our No. 1 player coming out in that draft club. That's part of the reason he'd been training with us, part of the reason we wanted him to come on the road. We wanted to see him day in and day out against some other pros, against some other top guys. Luke and I both felt he was ready because of his physical talent and then just his maturity and his dedication to his craft that he was going to be a longtime pro. I think everything was heading in that direction for him, and obviously that week he came up to Wisconsin had done really well at the league camp. Then, that Saturday night, it all ended."

July 23, 2016, is a day Kohl will never forget. A major rainstorm moved his entire camp inside. The punters and kickers could not get any work done because of the conditions. He leaned on Foltz that evening to help fill the void at the camp. Foltz grabbed a microphone and shared his story with the entire camp. It was one of the last things Foltz would do before the tragic accident that took his life later that evening. "I had seen Sam the night that he passed, and he was leaving with the other guys," Kohl said. "We all gave each other high-fives and said, 'We'll see you.' I gave him a big hug. He was just so happy, so smiling. It was a weird deal because we were at Coach Radke's house, and there was country music playing and guys just sitting around having a good talk. I just remember hearing a couple of big thunderstorms or thunder at night, just a big boom, and just thinking, *Man, that is really...*It was in that 15 to 20-minute period after they had left that the accident happened.

"I just remember thinking, *That's really like a bad, bad thunderstorm* because we dealt with rain that whole day... We were sitting there. There was loud music going, and I just remember hearing a couple of thunder and lightning bolts that just were different. Then we went to bed, and then I remember my wife waking me up at probably about 5:00 in the morning. I just remember that she had said that there's been an accident, and we think that two people had passed. Immediately, I had started waking up, and then we think it's Sam Foltz and Mike Sadler, and immediately a streak of cold adrenaline went from my spine, my neck, down my spinal cord, and I almost froze. I could not believe what I was hearing because I literally had been awake for maybe 15, 20 seconds. Then to hear those two names told to me, my first thought was those were the two most talented people in the whole camp. Of all the people that have passed—I didn't want anybody to die—but when I heard those two names, I immediately almost, I don't know what shock is, but I just remember feeling a shot of adrenaline right from basically my brain down through my spinal cord. It was the worst day of my life. It really truly was because we had to go through this deal where it hadn't become public yet.

"The police weren't announcing any names. We didn't know how to handle it. We didn't want to cancel camp because then everybody was going to ask. We weren't even for sure. In talking with Colby Delahoussaye [the lone survivor of that crash], he was on all types of drugs because of the pain from the accident, my wife had thought that it was potentially them. Then we had to get clearance at about 10:00 or 11:00 AM. Then once we got clearance as to who it was, and it was official, then we sent everybody home. We just said, 'Camp is over. You guys got to get going.' Mrs. Sadler flew in, and I talked to Gerald on the phone really for the first time in my life. Here's a guy that didn't even know me and he's comforting me in this situation. That's what I'm saying. I will say this: it was the worst day of my life, and Gerald Foltz helped me quite a bit through that because I had no idea how to handle that whole situation when that thing was breaking loose."

Hahn was in Kansas City, Missouri, to watch his cousin, Jake Deppen, pitch for the Royals. "A lot of our family was down there watching him. I remember Sunday morning getting up. We were waiting in the hotel lobby, and my mom gets a phone call and she gets off her phone and just collapsed to her knees and starts bawling. She just points at me and my girlfriend—now wife—and just points at us and tells us to come here. I'm like, *What?* She couldn't talk and she's bawling. I had in mind one of my friends from back home did something dumb just because I could tell it was that serious. I finally looked at her, yelled at her, and I was like, 'Mom, you have to say words. Tell me what's going on.' Then, yes, she told us…I was just numb. I didn't really say much. Then she told my sisters, and everybody started crying. I just really didn't want to touch anybody, kind of gave everybody an emotionless hug. I don't know. I just didn't really want to touch anybody.

"Then basically we get up and go home, go stop and eat in Platte City there at Culver's and just don't really say much. Then all the way home in my parents' vehicle, we all just took turns crying and said a couple of different things. Then we were going to go back to my house or at the farm there, and I was going to pack up and go. Then we actually went midway home. We decided to make a stop or just change course and go to Lincoln because we knew people were going to go to the stadium, and the guys were in town. We went to the stadium. They had the little vigil thing and just called one of my best friends from home and asked him to bring my pickup up with my stuff and just meet us there because we were going to start camp the next day and have Fan Day. Then we went over to his place and talked to Spencer [Lindsay] and Ryker [Fyfe], and Spencer stayed together there at Spencer and Sam's Place. Then we just went with it, just found out. Then at night I stayed back at the duplex that we lived in, didn't sleep, maybe slept four-to-five minutes, just couldn't, just laid there awake. Then, I remember coming in the next morning. Honestly, probably the best thing, we came in the next morning. I can't remember if we lifted—maybe a quick lift and then did a run—I remember just being so mad that they were making us do stuff, like do anything. Then as time went on and even the next day, the day after the next week in camp, the best thing they did was just make us go do something. They obviously knew that something significant happened, but they also knew the only way to mitigate it was just like you have to keep going and doing something. They handled that well."

Foltz was recruited by Pelini and played for him from 2012 to 2014. In 2015 he played for Mike Riley. It was a difficult situation for Riley to handle. There had never been a current player of the Huskers football team who had died during or before the start of the season. When quarterback Brook Berringer tragically passed in 1996, his NU career was over. Foltz's death happened days before the start of fall camp. He was likely going to be voted a team captain of the 2016 Huskers team. "I would definitely say that that is probably the best thing that Mike Riley did in his entire tenure was how he handled that situation," Hahn said. "The first day back was tough, and then Fan Day was tough. Then we showed up to practice. Honestly, it was tough on everyone, but everybody was just ready to work because they knew what, we just all knew what Sam would want. Sam would want to win and work...Obviously, you're going to mourn him and stuff like that, but he wouldn't want us like out there mourning him like crazy and not putting in the work to get better at football. We all knew that that wasn't him. The best thing that we could do to show our love and gratitude to him is to put our best effort forward on the field and get better."

* * *

Since the passing of Sam Foltz, many things have been done to remember his legacy. His family formed the Sam Foltz Foundation to give back to small communities to provide more opportunities for youth and those in need. Each year since 2021, Jamie Kohl and Spencer Lindsay have held a kicking camp in Foltz's honor. The inaugural event was held on farmland in Greeley, Nebraska, near Foltz's family farm around the five-year anniversary of his death.

The event was put on by the Foltz family and featured nearly 20 former Huskers players and more than 250 spectators and participants. That's especially impressive, considering the town of Greeley has a population of just 339. "This was kind of a unique situation," Kohl said in 2021. "We didn't know how many people were going to be here, and the community really came out and supported Sam. Hopefully, a couple of kids can take a few things they learned and work on them."

The event has since moved to Grand Island, Nebraska, and many former Huskers kickers and punters take part in it each year. In July of 2022, Nebraska's Department of Transportation dedicated a stretch of Highway 56 as the Sam Foltz Memorial Highway. This new memorial highway is near his family's home in Greeley.

The tributes and memorials for Foltz began in 2016. The Huskers opened the season that year against Fresno State at home. On Nebraska's opening punt, they took the field with just 10 players, receiving a delay of game penalty. The sold-out Memorial Stadium rose to their feet in applause. It had barely been a month since the passing of Foltz. "That was emotional," Sam Hahn said. "I don't think it would have mattered who we played that day. Our offense was going to go three-and-out that first drive because we did, because…it was almost just like something we needed to get done to move on with the game."

Throughout that season each week there was a different tribute to Foltz. When Oregon came to Memorial Stadium, they placed flowers on the 27-yard line in honor of Foltz. Illinois presented Nebraska with a Foltz Illini No. 27 jersey. Each week it was something different.

A commemorative coin featuring Foltz on one side and Mike Sadler on the other was used at the pregame coin toss of every Nebraska game in 2016. In 2018 the Sadler family and the Foltz family were honored at Memorial Stadium when Michigan State made its first trip since the tragic accident. In 2021 NU made its first trip to East Lansing, Michigan, since the 2016 accident, and both the Foltz and Sadler families were honored at midfield.

In August of 2017, Gerald Foltz even led world champion boxer Bud Crawford out wearing his son's No. 27 jersey before his fight against Julius Indongo at Pinnacle Bank Arena. Through it all, the Foltz family handled each situation with great strength. "Gerald is the guy that can put anybody at ease," Kohl said. "That's where Sam got a lot of it from. There's a lot of strange events that happened with Sam. I think a balloon landed at the 27-yard line…Gerald might have a story of like a bird or a dove or something at the 27-yard line. There's a lot of unique things surrounding Sam. Not to get too wild on you here, but Gerald had talked about a premonition he had had, and my mom had had one, too, prior to Sam's passing. I can't explain it all, but I think everything happens for a reason, and Sam Foltz is not like many people I've ever been around, ever, ever in my whole life. That whole year of going from stadium to stadium to stadium, I can't even explain it because a lot of those people I don't know how they knew Sam or didn't know Sam, but when it happened, it all of a sudden captured a whole stadium...People would send him emails and stuff and things would come up about Sam. I'm talking for at least probably 12, 18 months after his passing. He just somehow touched a lot of people."

Jill and Gerald Foltz traveled with the team for the entire 2016 season. They wanted to take every step their son would've taken. During pregame Gerald Foltz was known to stand in the northeast corner of Memorial Stadium. He would always give Sam a hug during warm-ups.

In 2016 he stood in that corner for every game to watch the specialists warm up. Instead of Sam giving him a hug, kicker Drew Brown was there for him every week. Brown was with Foltz in Wisconsin at the Kohl's Kicking Camp. He was the one who had to travel back to get Foltz's belongings after the accident.

The final thing Gerald attended was Nebraska's Pro Day in the spring of 2017, knowing that would've been his son's last duty as a Cornhusker. "Honestly, Gerald became Sam," Hahn said. "That's pretty much what it was. Your outlet to Sam was through Gerald. Gerald's outlet to Sam was through us. That's the way it is at every practice to this day, at every event to this day. Everybody's always going to find Gerald. It's just because Gerald's such a personality, too, and Sam mirrored that a little bit. I don't mean to be taking away anything from Jill or anything like that obviously because I love Jill. It's just like it's the guys' camaraderie connecting."

It's hard to know what type of pro career Foltz was destined for. In 2023 there were 96 specialists in the NFL between kickers, punters, and long snappers, and 75 of those 96 came through Kohl's events. Kohl would put Foltz's talents up there with anyone. In a time where the punting game has shifted to more of an Australian-style player, Foltz was Kohl's prize American prospect. He was true success story of a kid who grew up on a farm dreaming of playing for Nebraska. "Oh, man, no offense to any kickers, but you didn't look at Sam as a kicker," former Huskers assistant coach Rick Kaczenski said. "Sam was a guy that would jump in as a scout team receiver. Sam was a guy that on the sideline he'd get after guys. He was involved. He was a dude. That dude loved winning. That guy practices. He wanted to be the absolute best at his craft. His teammates were important to him; Nebraska was important to him. He was a guy. He wasn't a guy that went and took his footballs and went on another field and punted. He was involved in practice. He got on guys. Sam was an unbelievable guy. He's a guy you saw yourself coming back to campus and drinking a beer with years later. Just absolute tragedy still to this day.

"Those are things you just don't get over when you lose people like that. Losing anybody, but especially a guy like Sam and having kids, I don't know how you go on. I just really can't imagine. Yes, just gone too soon. That guy was a competitor. That guy wasn't about how far he could punt the football. That guy was about winning football games. *What can I do to help this team win football games?* You saw that, which is really difficult to do from a kicker. That's hard to prove to your teammates, and he proved it to every single staff member and every single teammate how important his job was and how important winning, how important helping the football team be successful was. That's difficult to do as a kicker, but he accomplished that."

PART 5

THE RIVALRIES

17

Oklahoma

No rivalry defines Nebraska football more than Oklahoma. For nearly 30 seasons, the game had a major impact on the college football season—no different than Michigan vs. Ohio State or Alabama vs. Georgia has today. Just think about this: the famed 1971 Game of the Century had a TV viewing audience of 55 million for the ABC broadcast on Thanksgiving Day.

The rivalry changed forever in 1996 when the two schools joined the Big 12 Conference. Before that it was locked into Black Friday to close out the Big 8 season. For some reason the leaders of the new Big 12 made a very questionable decision regarding protecting the OU vs. NU rivalry. "There's no question that the vaporization of the Nebraska–Oklahoma game was terribly detrimental to Nebraska," former Nebraska play-by-play voice and historian Jim Rose said. "Not having that rival played every year was very, very damaging to Nebraska. Rivals motivate. Rivals motivate coaches, rivals motivate players, rivals motivate donors, rivals motivate the media. Losing Oklahoma was a huge setback for Nebraska football. The Big 12 Conference would not preserve that rival. If you look at it, they preserved every other rivalry in the merger between the Big 8 and the Southwest Conference except Nebraska and Oklahoma. They preserved Oklahoma State–Oklahoma, they preserved Texas against all the Texas schools, they preserved Texas–Oklahoma, they preserved Kansas–Missouri, they preserved Kansas State–Kansas. They preserved every one of them except Nebraska–Oklahoma because they knew if Nebraska loses its rival, that's a setback, and it was."

Like all great rivalries, the Sooners and the Huskers took some time to develop. Before Tom Osborne, Bob Devaney, Barry Switzer, and Chuck Fairbanks, there was an era under Bud Wilkinson where Oklahoma dominated not only Nebraska, but also everyone in college football.

In 1959 when OU came to Lincoln, they had a 74-game conference winning streak and had won 14 straight league titles from 1946 to 1959. They had beaten the Huskers 16 straight times and won the national championship in 1950, 1955, and 1956. When Nebraska beat Oklahoma in 1959, it was not only the greatest upset in program history, but also the moment that woke up Huskers fans and set the stage for Bob Devaney to come to NU in 1962.

When you think of great rivalries in college football, generally there is a form of hatred on both sides. Today, Nebraska fans feel that way when the Huskers play Iowa. It used to be that way at times with Colorado and Texas. That's what made the rivalry with Oklahoma so unique.

There was deep mutual respect from the coaches to the players and the fans.

To this day, it's not uncommon to see Switzer do an event with Osborne or to see Billy Sims and Johnny Rodgers chopping it up at the Heisman ceremony in New York. "It was unusual because when you think about Ohio State, Michigan, and Woody Hayes saying that he wouldn't even buy gas in Michigan," Osborne said, "then Bill McCartney, when he came from Michigan to coach at Colorado, I think he decided that in order to have a good team, you had to have a rival, and it had to be nasty. I never quite understood that. I never reciprocated some of the antics that eventually started coming from Colorado. A lot of that was because we felt that Oklahoma was probably as intense a football rivalry as any place in the country mainly because, I think, for about a 30-year period either Nebraska or Oklahoma won the conference championship 29 times. It was a legitimate rivalry based on accomplishment on the field."

If you followed football in the 1970s and 1980s, you probably spent your Thanksgiving weekend watching the Sooners and the Huskers. Very few college football games were televised in that era, making Oklahoma and Nebraska a bigger showcase every year. "Every time you played Oklahoma, you heard from people back home that either watched or were saying they were going to watch," former Huskers defensive back Jimmy Burrow said. "Even as you got into the pros, whether it was when I played with the Packers for the year or the CFL, teammates said, 'Oh, yes, I watched Nebraska–Oklahoma every year' because most of the time they weren't playing on that day. There might have been another game or two, but there weren't many when Nebraska–Oklahoma played. The coaching staffs were really good friends. Warren Powers, Monte Kiffin, and Jim Walden were close with the Oklahoma guys and Coach Switzer and Larry Lacewell. My understanding is even the night before games that they would hang out. I used to hear they would get together and have dinner at the Legion Club. Everybody, I think, understood that you were playing against the best, and the coaches were coaching against the best. As I said, there was so much at stake in those games. That's certainly one of my disappointments that I never was on a team that beat Oklahoma. I was a part of it with Coach Solich when my son Jamie and the guys beat Oklahoma that day in Lincoln when Eric Crouch caught the reverse pass for a touchdown. I did have a victory under my belt but not when I played."

For Osborne, Oklahoma was a hurdle he struggled to get past, especially when Switzer led the Sooners. He started his career at NU 1–8 against Oklahoma before he was able to win three in a row from 1981 to 1983. In a lot of ways, that was a turning point for Osborne at Nebraska. Even when he got his first win against Switzer in 1978, he dealt with the setback of losing to Missouri and then having to face OU again in the Orange Bowl and losing 31–24. "The fans weren't real sure because we lost to Oklahoma the first five times that I had coached teams against [Switzer], and [it] had become a one-game season," Osborne said. "We'd win nine or 10 games, but if we didn't beat Oklahoma, we had a bad year. It was not easygoing, but eventually we did beat Oklahoma in '78, and then things got better after that. I survived the curse of following a very popular, very successful coach, but a lot of times it's pretty touch and go."

Former offensive lineman Barney Cotton remembers that first win for Osborne against Oklahoma in 1978. "It was a big deal for us and it was a big deal for him," Cotton said. It was interesting because in a hallway the week of Oklahoma, he asked me, 'What do you think? Do you think we should maybe take the pads off this week, kind of shorten practice?'

"I looked right at him. I said, 'You know what, Coach? I think we should prepare for Oklahoma exactly the same way we prepared for every team we played this year. I wouldn't change anything. Leave the pads on, the same length of practice. Let's just prepare for these guys the same way and let's go get it.' He goes, 'You know, Barney, I think you might have a pretty good idea there.' It was interesting because he was standing there in the north end zone when he had that little locker room by the training room down there. We had a great talk. I think it's maybe on a Sunday after we beat Kansas, but it meant a lot to me that he just asked me a question off the cuff like getting ready to play Oklahoma...I'll always remember that. That's what we did. We didn't do anything different that week. Then we went out and played really well. We played really physical. Then the unfortunate thing about it is we went and peed down our leg the next week. We were all set. It was like a No. 3 vs. No. 2, and that was set up to be No. 2 vs. No. 1, and we got beat so then we ended up getting Oklahoma for a rematch in the Orange Bowl."

Former Huskers running back Tony Davis (1972–75) has a much more honest view of playing the Sooners in the early Osborne years: there was nothing magical about the Sooners and what they did. OU just had elite talent. "During my era we couldn't get over the hump with Oklahoma," Davis said. "They were just better than we were. That's all there was to it. People say, 'No, we didn't play well against them.' Well, you know what? They were pretty freaking good. I played the last game, I think, with all three Selmon brothers on the defensive line for Oklahoma. We never crossed the 50-yard line. We were ranked fifth in the country. We never crossed the 50-yard line. That's how good their defense was. They just shut our ass down. We couldn't do anything. They were good, and that was discouraging to all of us, including the fans."

Guy Ingles played in the Nebraska–Oklahoma series as a receiver and was also part of Osborne's coaching staff. He said the criticism Osborne received early in his career was tough because OU had some of the best teams in college football for that era. "From '73 to '78, we didn't beat them. We didn't beat them in '72, but by the time '72 rolled around, they'd been in the wishbone for two years, and they had people coming out of their ears," Ingles said. "If you watch any of those backfields warm up and run that wishbone in a pregame, you'd be scared to death. They were the four fastest guys on the field."

The turning point for the series for Osborne was the addition of Turner Gill at quarterback. Osborne won a key recruiting battle against the Sooners to convince the Texas native Gill to drive past Norman, Oklahoma, and play for the Huskers. Gill was ahead of his time. He was considered one of college football's first great dual-threat quarterbacks. Gill was the weapon Osborne needed to beat Switzer three games in a row from 1981 to 1983.

Before Gill, Osborne had quarterbacks who could throw but weren't great runners. Gill gave them both, which made the wrinkle of the option a perfect counter against Switzer's wishbone attack. "He was a dual-threat quarterback," Osborne said. "He was legitimately a very good passer and he was a good runner and very stable guy. I think he was in his sophomore year and I told him I wanted him to start, and he said he wasn't ready. About the middle, after first three or four games, he decided he would start. He had a great career for us, but we didn't really just go to option football when Turner came. We'd had some really good throwing quarterbacks. We had David Humm in the early '70s. It was '72, '73, '74, and then we had Vince Ferragamo, and both those guys had pretty long NFL careers as NFL-type quarterbacks, but we struggled with a running quarterback and stopping them in Oklahoma particularly. We had Tom Sorley and we had Jeff Quinn, so we had some guys that could run the option pretty well. Then, of course, Turner came along and he was probably the best of that group. It's really hard to find a guy that's a really good runner and really good passer."

The back and forth between Switzer and Osborne from 1973 to 1988 is what defined this series. In great rivalries both teams have their moments. At times Osborne had his, but Switzer would always find an answer. "The shit he's gone through...They have no idea," Davis said of Switzer. "Yet he shares with his former players and players like Coach Osborne does his. They're polar opposites, but they have a great deal of respect for each other. In fact, Coach Switzer told me, 'Beating Coach Osborne made me the coach I am today. Losing to Coach Osborne made me the coach I am today.' He says, 'That rivalry we had made us both great coaches.'"

* * *

A Sugar Bowl snub in 1971 fueled Bob Devaney heading into the Game of the Century, which was a program-defining game for Nebraska. That contest delivered the greatest individual moment in program history—Johnny Rodgers' 72-yard punt return for a touchdown. For whatever reason, though, the Sugar Bowl organizers thought Oklahoma was the better team and would win the 1971 game against the Huskers. They hedged their bet and extended the Sooners an invite before kickoff. Devaney got wind of this and was furious.

This fueled Devaney heading into the game, and he let the Sugar Bowl folks know his thoughts after the 35–31 win against the Sooners. "He had a temper now, and don't anybody ever tell you any different," former Nebraska assistant coach Jim Walden said. "He was a delightful man whom I will respect till I die. Don't ever think he didn't have a temper, and he knew how to use it at the right time. I'll never forget this as we're coming up the ramp after the game. Now we've won the game of the year, no doubt about it, think about it. Think of the joy: 35–31. It was a magnificent gameday, Thanksgiving Day, Game of the Century, we're coming up the ramp. [Assistant] Warren Powers and I couldn't hug each other enough. We're coming up the ramp, and as we get to the door of the dressing room, there are two Sugar Bowl representatives talking to Bob. Or they're just about to as we start to walk by. They had made a decision—the Sugar Bowl—and I don't know why Bob wanted to go to the Sugar Bowl...maybe [because] we've been to the Orange Bowl three times, but the Sugar Bowl came out and made the statement that they felt Oklahoma was the better team and they were going to offer Oklahoma the invitation prior to the game. In other words, Oklahoma had accepted the invitation to the Sugar Bowl prior to the game."

Interestingly, Devaney knew all of this going into the Game of the Century but chose to keep the information to himself. That was his style. He didn't want it to distract his team. "He never said a word in the staff meeting. Normally, you'd think he would've been mad," Walden said. "I would've have come and said: 'Those sons of a bitch Sugar Bowl people, they think their team's better than ours!' We had no knowledge other than the fact that we saw in the paper that Sugar Bowl had invited Oklahoma. We were so busy we didn't think about that being a slight at the time. I don't even think I gave it a thought. Okay, so we're coming up to the locker room and, just as we swing around here, we hear him say to those two Sugar Bowl guys, 'You can take your fucking Sugar Bowl and shove it up your ass. I don't care if we ever go there, but don't you ever try to put my team down.' They're both standing there just like you had just been whipped and verbally thrashed by your father. They just look like two whipped dogs, and Warren and I look at each other—and I'll never forget—he says to me, 'Hell, I didn't want to go the Sugar Bowl the rest of my life anyway.' Because that was our first thought. It's like, 'Oh my God, he's telling the Sugar Bowl people to kiss his ass, take your bowl, and shove it up your ass.' It's like, 'Oh my God, Bob, we'll never get invited to the Sugar Bowl.'

"I leave there in 1972. We go to the Orange Bowl. After that game the next year, we end up going to the Orange Bowl and beat Alabama. The next year go to the Orange Bowl again and beat Notre Dame. Now, after he had screamed at those two Sugar Bowl representatives, guess where they went in '74? To the Sugar Bowl. I'm just telling you things that would make him mad, that would eat at him, but he wouldn't share it. In other words, he didn't. He had the ability to carry his own grudge. And down deep I knew in my heart the way he was talking—*I knew*—that had been on his mind. If we won the game, he was going to lay into their ass. He was unique in that sense, but, boy, he was mad. I'm thinking, *We just won the biggest game of our lives, and you're out here chewing these guys from the Sugar Bowl's ass.*"

18

Colorado

WHEN BILL MCCARTNEY ARRIVED IN COLORADO FROM Michigan in 1982, he wanted the Buffaloes to have an earmarked rivalry game. From 1979 to 1981, CU had won a combined seven games. There was not a lot going for the Buffs at that time. Meanwhile, McCartney came from Michigan, where the Wolverines had an established rivalry game every year with Ohio State. That defined their season in many cases.

The Big 8 at that time also had one of those games—Nebraska vs. Oklahoma. From 1962 to 1988, Nebraska or Oklahoma won or shared a piece of the Big 8 championship. OU and NU played in a combined 20 Orange Bowls, where the Big 8 champion was generally sent, during that period. It was their league. It was called the Big Two and the Little Six Conference. That's why Tom Osborne had difficulty understanding his logic when McCartney took over at CU and dubbed the Cornhuskers their new rivalry game.

Nobody understands Colorado football and its history better than Dave Plati. He started as a student at CU in 1978 and was their head sports information director beginning in 1984, becoming the youngest SID in the nation at that time. He retired from Colorado officially in August of 2023 after a 45-year career. He was on the ground floor of the Colorado vs. Nebraska rivalry and said a lot of it was a misunderstanding that took on a life of its own.

What struck McCartney was how Osborne ran the Cornhuskers program and how great the fanbase was. Players graduated, NU led the nation in Academic All-Americans, and it had one of the most loyal fanbases in the country. He saw it first-hand in 1982 when the Cornhuskers faithful took over his stadium in their first meeting. Nebraska won that game in Boulder, Colorado, 40–14. "McCartney was shocked at how much red was in the stadium, and that's where it was born out of, why he picked Nebraska to be the rival," Plati said. "Nebraskans took it the wrong way. If any fans should have been pissed off, it should have been Oklahoma's fans because when McCartney picked a rival he said you picked a winning program that had done things the right way that was graduating the players. I don't think he meant it as an unveiled shot at Oklahoma, but he really was complimenting the Nebraska program to emulate them, as he wanted us to be like Nebraska. I think people just took that the wrong way. He never had any hatred for Nebraska. McCartney always had some respect for them."

Osborne had a different view. "A lot of our fans were from North Platte out west. It's just as close to go to Boulder as it was to Lincoln and, of course, some from this end of the state, too, but tickets were available out there, and we sold a lot," Osborne said. "That became a real sticking point for Bill McCartney. He did not like Nebraska fans out there."

From 1968 to 1985, Nebraska won 18 games in a row against Colorado. It's hard to dub an opponent a rival when the series is that one-sided. Things finally took a turn in 1986 when CU knocked off No. 3 ranked Nebraska 20–10 in Boulder. "That was the turning point of our program of the McCartney era," Plati said.

From that point on, the rivalry began. The Denver media was interested. Sports talk radio in Denver began making fun of Nebraskans. *The Denver Post* columnist Woody Paige also became a key voice in the rivalry and was often critical of Osborne and the Huskers program.

McCartney even played into it, famously saying he'd "rather be dead than red." "It started in the late '80s, in the mid-'80s, on talk radio out here with Nebraska jokes," Plati said. "A couple of them were funny. When they started making fun of farming and growing corn, and you're like, 'They're feeding the freaking nation. What's wrong with you?' I think Woody Paige might have been starting up with his columns and the sports talk show in Denver because Denver had sports talk radio before most cities in the country...The constant jokes were getting under Nebraska's skin because they were insulting to the population. We're like, 'Guys, you're not helping us.'"

Osborne concurred. "Some of the peripheral stuff, the Nebraska jokes, and that kind of stuff," he said, "I never did quite understand."

Colorado is known for Ralphie, the live Buffalo mascot that runs onto the field before each home game. He does it again before the teams take the field in the second half. There was a legendary picture from the 1995 game in Boulder, where Osborne and his team were waiting to come out to the field, and Ralphie charged right toward them. Osborne yelled at Ralphie and his handlers to get out of their way. "The only other thing I think that Nebraska did to get under our skin," Plati said, "was Osborne would complain about Ralphie running."

Nebraska has a rule in their stadium that live game mascots are not allowed. It was mainly put into place to keep Ralphie out of Lincoln. "A lot of places are like that," Plati said. "We eventually—from a risk management standpoint here after [Oklahoma linebacker] Brian Bosworth went out there acting like he was going to block Ralphie and then dived out of the way for his life—we started taking the field first so that Ralphie would be in the trailer before the opponents took the field."

* * *

By the late 1980s, Oklahoma's football program began to fall after Barry Switzer left, and the Sooners were placed on NCAA probation in 1989. This opened the door for Colorado to move up a slot in the Big 8 and play several meaningful games with Nebraska. From 1987 to 1996, the Colorado vs. Nebraska game was a ranked-on-ranked matchup. In 1989–90 CU became the only Big 8 school to beat Osborne two years in a row besides Oklahoma, Iowa State, and Missouri.

By 1989 the Buffaloes became a national power. They beat the No. 3 Huskers 27–21 and lost to Notre Dame in the Orange Bowl for the national championship. The next year, 1990, is when some real juice started in the rivalry. It was one of the most flawed national championship scenarios ever seen in college football. Colorado split the title that year with Georgia Tech. However, the Buffs were far from perfect. They tied Tennessee to open the season, lost at Illinois, and edged out Notre Dame 10–9 in the Orange Bowl after Rocket Ismail's punt return in the fourth quarter was called back on a clip.

Meanwhile, Nebraska lost to Colorado 27–12 in 1990. The Huskers were blown out on Black Friday against an unranked Oklahoma team 45–10. The season ended on a low point, as the No. 19 Huskers were then sent to the Citrus Bowl to play No. 2 ranked Georgia Tech. The Yellow Jackets, who finished the year 11–0–1, dominated Nebraska 45–21. Tech's best wins were against 10–2 Clemson and 8–4 Virginia, who finished No. 9 and No. 23 in the final polls, respectively. Georgia Tech tied a North Carolina team that finished unranked and 6–4–1.

Colorado beat Southwest Conference champion Texas and Pac-10 champion Washington, tied SEC champion Tennessee, and lost to coBig Ten champions Illinois. The Buffaloes also ran the table in the Big 8 Conference and beat No. 5 Notre Dame in the Orange Bowl. It ranks as one of the toughest schedules in college football history. Still, there was question. One of CU's wins came on a controversial play, where the Buffaloes were awarded an extra down that helped them win at Missouri. The contest was famously dubbed the "Fifth Down Game."

They, though, took care of business and won the Orange Bowl against Notre Dame while Georgia Tech did its part and handled the Huskers in Orlando, Florida. The Buffs were voted No. 1 in the AP poll, receiving 39 out of 60 votes. However, in the UPI coach's poll, the Yellow Jackets edged out Colorado by one vote. The final ballots were never made public, but it was confirmed that Tom Osborne did not vote for Colorado as No. 1. He put the Yellow Jackets ahead of them on his ballot, costing McCartney and the Buffs the outright national championship. "People blamed Tom Osborne in 1990 for not voting for Colorado and causing us to split national championship with Georgia Tech," Plati said. "We know he didn't vote us No. 1. We do know that for sure. Technically, if he votes us No. 2 and Georgia Tech No. 1, well, that's because we lost by one point.

Yes, if you flop it, we win by one point. I've heard through the years he voted us third or fourth. UPI never told us. The point I've always made is it's not like UPI called him and said, 'Look, you're the last guy voting. What are you going to do?' To blame Tom directly for that, I think always was a little bit unfair."

After 1991 Nebraska would win nine games in a row against Colorado. From 1996 to 2000, every game was decided by five points or fewer. It was a competitive rivalry, but the Huskers had the upper hand when it mattered. The defining moment came in 1994 when Brook Berringer led No. 2 Nebraska to a 24–7 victory against No. 3 Colorado. It was virtually a college football semifinal playoff game, as the winner had the inside track to play for the national championship. ESPN's *College GameDay* was on hand in Lincoln. That was the first full season *GameDay* went on location. The 1993 Florida State vs. Notre Dame game was the show's first ever live remote showcase and only one of that season. ESPN came to Lincoln for two of their six live remotes in 1994, and Colorado was loaded that year. It was arguably Bill McCartney's best team. He had quarterback Kordell Stewart, running back Rashaan Salaam, and wide receiver Michael Westbrook. Salaam would go on to win the Heisman Trophy in 1994, Westbrook was a consensus first-team All-American, and Stewart was a second-team, AP All-American. Earlier that season the Buffs won road games at No. 4 Michigan and No. 16 Texas and had beaten No. 10 Wisconsin in Boulder.

The Huskers were without Tommie Frazier at quarterback, which appeared to give Colorado an advantage on paper. Instead, Osborne and Berringer delivered a masterful game in the 200th consecutive sellout in Memorial Stadium history. "Elliot Uzelac, our offensive coordinator, wanted to beat Nebraska at their game by just pounding the ball," Plati said. "Michael Westbrook to this day is pissed off because we never threw the ball deep. We had all those receivers on the team. We had four really good receivers. We never threw deep on Nebraska's secondary... Maybe it wasn't a weakness, but it was a very average secondary. We never even tried it. So that pissed off a lot of the wide receivers to this day."

The win set up Osborne to win his first national title, as the Huskers beat Miami in the Orange Bowl 24–17. Colorado finished 11–1 and No. 3, beating Notre Dame in the Fiesta Bowl 41–24.

The next century featured another game that impacted the national landscape of college football in 2001. The Buffs were a sneaky 8–2 team heading into Black Friday and ranked No. 14 in the AP poll. Nebraska was 11–0 and ranked No. 2. However, the Huskers needed to beat CU to win the Big 12 North division. Colorado's two losses were to a David Carr-led Fresno State team and Big 12 South division winner Texas.

The North was still on the line in Boulder, Colorado, and Gary Barnett's Buffs came out swinging. They won the game 62–36, as running back Chris Brown ran for six touchdowns. "The thing about 62–36 was we were still 6–1 in the Big 12 but stubbed our toe in the season opener at Fresno State," Plati said. "We went down to Texas, and they waxed us in the first meeting. I think people thought we were a good team. We were still No. 14, but we had two losses heading into Nebraska. When we went up 35–3 in the second quarter, I think the football world was shocked because I know in the press box we were just going, 'What the hell's going on here?' They climbed back into that game. It was 42–30 at one point. It was not a given that we were going to win that after they started chipping away. I think they fumbled deep in the end...if I recall...I think they fumbled at the 1-yard line when it was 42–23."

The significance of that game is that Nebraska's program has never been the same since. The Huskers still backdoored into the BCS national championship game, losing to Miami in the Rose Bowl. But since those losses to the Buffs and Hurricanes, Nebraska's program heading into the 2025 season has only been ranked in the AP top five for one week, and that day in Boulder changed the trajectory of the Cornhuskers program. They had never experienced a loss of that magnitude in the program's modern era.

* * *

The other interesting thing about this game over the years is its impact on head coaches and their futures. In 1978 Tom Osborne was beginning to feel pressure at Nebraska, as he started his career at Nebraska 1–6 against Oklahoma. He lost to the Sooners for the national championship during the 1978 season. CU courted Osborne for the head coach opening after Bill Mallory stepped down. Osborne came to Boulder, Colorado, and interviewed for the position. He toured the campus, and some thought he might take the job. CU offered him a reported $100,000 annual salary—three times the base salary he received at NU. Ultimately, he stayed at Nebraska, and the Buffs hired Chuck Fairbanks before Bill McCartney took over in 1982.

Over the years the game impacted several other head coaching moves between the two schools. In 2003 Frank Solich was fired after he beat the Buffaloes to finish 9–3. It was unheard of to fire a nine-win college football coach then. After the 2005 season, Colorado fired Gary Barnett when Nebraska went into Boulder and blew out the Buffs 30–3 in the famous Bill Callahan "Restore the Order" game. CU was beaten 70–3 by eventual national champion Texas in the Big 12 title game the next week.

Barnett was fired after the game. "Just to go out and be able to have the performance we had on offense in that game," former Nebraska quarterback and Cincinnati Bengal head coach Zac Taylor said, "Gary Barnett, I didn't think very fondly of that team at that time."

When Taylor was in high school, Barnett pulled his initial scholarship offer to CU. "He got fired, I think, a game after that," Taylor said.

In 2007 Callahan lost to Colorado 65–51 in Boulder. The loss kept the Huskers from playing in a bowl game. Osborne fired Callahan the next morning. The 2010 game was the final time the two schools would meet as conference opponents, and Nebraska won 45–17 with backup quarterback Cody Green under center. Colorado fired head coach Dan Hawkins after his team failed to qualify for a bowl game for the third consecutive year.

In recent years, the two schools have done their best to rekindle the rivalry's flame, meeting in 2018 and 2019 and 2023 and 2024. The 2018 game in Lincoln was Scott Frost's first as Nebraska's head coach. His team blew a fourth-quarter lead as quarterback Adrian Martinez's leg was maliciously twisted after a play by Buffs linebacker Jacob Callier. The injury kept him out the next week against Troy, and the Huskers lost that game 24–19, as they were forced to start a walk-on at quarterback. That setback with Martinez played a big part in Nebraska's 0–6 start to the Frost era.

Then, in 2019 Nebraska blew a 17–0 halftime lead in Boulder and fell 34–31. The Buffs were not a great team in 2019, finishing 5–7. The win's significance was that you could argue it helped boost Mel Tucker's stock enough in his first year at Colorado to land the Michigan State job in 2020. That game was also the beginning of the end for Frost, as his team blew the lead in Boulder with more than 60 percent of the stadium filled with Nebraska fans. It also is the last week Nebraska was ranked in the AP poll until it beat Colorado during the 2024 season.

The 2023 season delivered another interesting page to the rivalry, as new Nebraska head coach Matt Rhule faced Deion Sanders in Boulder. It was Sanders' first home game as head coach. It drew the largest crowd at CU since 2008. Sanders called the game with NU "personal" after accusing Rhule of criticizing how he unloaded the Buffs 2022 roster and then refilled it with more than 60 transfer portal additions.

Then, during pregame of the 2023 game, Sanders' son, Shedeur, accused Rhule and Nebraska of disrespecting the Buffalo at the 50-yard line when they entered Folsom Field. Rhule would later say they just conducted their standard routine of praying in reflection before entering the locker room. "We do it at every stadium," Rhule said. "We go there and we pray for blessings. When [Colorado's players] came in, I asked them if they wanted to [join]. I asked Shedeur if he wanted to pray with us. I pray over every field. I'm a public official, but I can have my own faith. When I say pray, we take a moment as a team. We have Muslim guys; we have non-believers. We just take a moment as a team, and I just want that field to be safe for everybody. No one's going to tell me who I am.

"At the end of the game, they told me, 'Hey, we're going to run right off the field. They're going to storm the field.' I said, 'Absolutely not. Absolutely not. Absolutely not.' I don't care if I get beaten up by a mob; I'm running across that field and I'm shaking Coach [Deion] Sanders' hand. When you're losing, people are going to say all kinds of things about you. I know exactly who I am. I know exactly who I am. And I'm coaching this team with class and I'm not changing. And I went over there and I shook that man's hand. I whispered in his ear. I've never disrespected an opponent a day in my life and never will."

Shedeur Sanders had his own take on the mid-field incident. "It was extremely personal," he said after his team's 36–14 win in 2023. "We go out there and warm up, you've got the head coach of the other team trying to stand out in the middle of the Buff. It's okay if a couple players do it; it's fine. Just enjoy the scenery. But when you've got the whole team trying to disrespect it, I'm not going for that at all. I went in there and disrupted it. So they knew I'm for real. The Buffaloes mean a lot to me. Personally, that's what I was saying pregame and that's when I knew it was just extreme disrespect."

Even with Nebraska and Colorado's programs being nowhere near what they used to be, the 2018, 2019, and 2023 games were all nationally televised on either FOX or ABC. The 2023 game in Boulder drew 8.73 million viewers on FOX, accounting for the most people watching a Nebraska football game on TV since the 2009 Big 12 Championship Game had 8.98 million viewers. Nebraska got the last word in the rivalry with its 28–10 win in Lincoln in 2024. That victory, which drew 5.67 million viewers on FOX, led to the first field storming at Memorial Stadium since beating No. 2 Colorado in 1994. It also put the Huskers back into the top 25 for the first time since losing to CU in 2019.

19

Texas

IN 1996 NEBRASKA WAS ON TOP OF THE COLLEGE FOOTBALL mountain. The Huskers dominated the Big 8 conference and just captured their second straight national championship. The Big 8 had a setup built to give their teams a recruiting advantage. Big 8 schools benefited from conference admission standards that allowed them to take partial academic qualifiers. It was an advantage that helped schools like Oklahoma, Nebraska, and Colorado add players to their rosters other leagues would not allow. NU also had two built-in rivalries by 1996—the traditional rivalry game with Oklahoma and its newly formed one against Colorado.

When the Big 8 Conference merged with Texas, Texas A&M, Texas Tech, and Baylor in 1996 to form the Big 12, the Huskers nearly lost everything. Their annual game with Oklahoma on Black Friday was taken away because the Big 12 formed a North and a South division. "It was a shame because we wanted and we lobbied pretty hard to continue, but they decided to go with the North and South division," former head coach and athletic director Tom Osborne said. "Of course, in the Big Ten, we have different divisions, but still some teams will play cross-division every year simply because of rivalry. You didn't have to structure it where Oklahoma would only play Nebraska two years out of every four. We were trying very hard to maintain that relationship. I think Oklahoma said, 'Well, we'll just play the South division.' Of course, Texas was a big rival for them, too. I think that was an opening crack. The structure going from Big 8 to Big 12, that probably was not the wisest decision. I think if Oklahoma and Nebraska continued to play, it would've been better."

The newly formed Big 12 conference also voted to eliminate allowing schools to recruit partial academic qualifiers. It even voted 11–1 to add a conference championship game. That was one of the key revenue pieces the newly formed league was able to add by going to 12 teams and two divisions. The SEC was the first Football Bowl Subdivision league to have a championship game when it added South Carolina and Arkansas in 1992.

Almost all these decisions were driven by one school—Texas. The Longhorns built the newly formed Big 12 Conference to benefit them. The rest of the Big 8 was also tired of Nebraska dominating during that era and they voted right along with Texas. In many ways, Osborne knew the challenges Nebraska's new conference would add. They lost out on academic partial qualifiers and now had to win an extra game in December to play for a national championship.

Coincidentally, NU's first matchup with Texas started a rivalry in the Big 12 both on and off the field. It was a rivalry that ultimately led to Nebraska leaving the Big 12 for the Big Ten due to the Longhorns and five other Big 12 schools looking to merge with the Pac-10 to form a 16-team super conference. That never happened, but the damage was done, and Nebraska, Colorado, Missouri, and Texas A&M all left the Big 12 in 2011 and 2012 to start the realignment carousel in college football. It was a war in which Texas fired the first shot and changed the landscape of Nebraska football forever.

* * *

In the mid-1990s, the Southwest Conference was a mess. Texas A&M could not compete on the national landscape, Arkansas had left for the SEC, and Texas was not considered a national power. The league needed a change. Several other teams in the SWC were put on NCAA probation during that period. The Big 8 offered them a fresh start with plenty of teams winning at a high level. In the final year of the Big 8, Nebraska (1), Colorado (5), Kansas State (7), and Kansas (9) all finished ranked in the AP top 10. Over an 11-year period, the Big 8 captured four national championships from 1985 to 1995.

The Southwest Conference had not won a national championship since 1970. "The Southwest Conference was really struggling," Osborne said. "They had, I think, probably three or four teams that were on probation. There'd been a lot of cheating down there. I know some of those teams were drawing 20,000 fans, and things had really gone south. I think the Big 8 saw that maybe by adding some teams you could have more TV inventory. We—the coaches in the Big 8—were told that we were accepting them in and we didn't need to take them.

"They needed us more than we needed them because the Southwest Conference was really in bad shape. I remember Carl James, the commissioner of the Big 8 at that time, telling me that they would be brought in and would play under Big 8 rules. In other words, conferences sometimes had individual rules academically. For instance, we had the ability to take the Prop 48's and they didn't. It was our understanding that when they came into the league it would all be Big 8 rules. For some reason, they had a meeting of the presidents of the various universities. They came up with an entirely different plan. I remember asking [Nebraska chancellor] Graham Spanier, 'What in the world went on?' We we're supposed to play by Big 8 rules.' He said, 'Well, we felt sorry for them.'"

Osborne almost had to take a step back when Spanier said that. "I said, 'Well, why would you do that?' One thing led to another," Osborne said. "First of all, we had the Big 12 Championship Game, and it was going to be played in Kansas City. Then all of a sudden, it goes to Dallas. The headquarters of the Big 8 were in Kansas City. That's where the headquarters of the Big 12 were. Then, all of a sudden, that went to Dallas. It seemed it went in the Southwest Conference. I think Texas, for whatever reason, was in an ascendant position where they were calling the shots. They assumed when they went in the Big 12 that that would continue in the Big 12. It was always a little bit uneasy situation where we didn't feel the same sense of comradery, whereas in the Big 8, I thought there was a pretty good, healthy mutual respect among the people. It wasn't quite that way in the Big 12."

On the field, when Nebraska and Texas played, the Huskers were often considered the favorite, especially in some of the early meetings. However, for whatever reason, the Longhorns always had the Huskers' number. The two teams played 10 times in the Big 12 from 1996 to 2010. UT went 9–1 in those meetings. No school dominated Nebraska more in the Big 12 than Texas. In 1996 and 1999, the Longhorns cost the Huskers a chance at playing for a national championship. During the 1996 Big 12 title game, several Huskers players came down with the flu the day of the game, and Texas won 37–27. It cost Nebraska a chance to play Florida State in the Sugar Bowl for a national championship. Florida then got a shot at the Seminoles and won the game 52–20 in a rematch for the two in-state rivals.

In 1999 Nebraska traveled to Austin, Texas, and lost to UT 24–20 in what was dubbed "the Fumble Game." NU had three costly fumbles, including one at the goal line by running back Correll Buckhalter in the fourth quarter in what would've been the go-ahead touchdown. The Huskers would go on to beat Texas 22–6 in the Big 12 Championship later that season but still were denied an opportunity to play for the national title with an 11–1 record. NU finished No. 3 in the final BCS poll behind Florida State and Virginia Tech.

In 1998 the Longhorns would win in Memorial Stadium, 20–16 to snap Nebraska's 47-game home winning streak. The win catapulted Texas running back Ricky Williams to the Heisman Trophy, as it was NU's first home loss since September 21, 1991, which came against national champion Washington. "We couldn't understand why Texas had our number," former Huskers All-American cornerback Ralph Brown said in 2013. "They broke our home winning streak, and then we go back up there, and they beat us again. They just had our number. I don't know why we couldn't beat them. I was just so glad we beat them my senior year [in 1999] when it counted, but they did have our number, and we just couldn't figure it out. We were more talented than they were, but the ball ended up bouncing their way when the game was on the line. That's something that angers me to this day because that's what they have over us."

But it was the 2009 game with Texas that arguably changed the path of the program. When Nebraska played Texas in that

Big 12 Championship Game at the Dallas Cowboys' stadium in Arlington, Texas, it was a 14-point underdog. The Longhorns were undefeated and led by Heisman Trophy finalist Colt McCoy. Meanwhile, the Huskers were winning ugly with elite defense, special teams play, and an offense that was not built to put up points or yards. Nobody gave the Big Red a chance vs. Texas heading into the game. The Longhorns had put up 40-plus points in eight of their 12 games.

NU had lost games earlier that season at Virginia Tech and then at home against Iowa State and Texas Tech. It easily could've won all three of them, so its 9–3 record heading into Dallas was somewhat misleading. The Huskers had the nation's best defensive player in Ndamukong Suh and arguably the best overall defense in the country. They delivered a defensive performance for the ages as the clock initially expired with the Huskers on top 12–10. NU's defense sacked McCoy nine times in the game and held his high-powered offense to just 202 yards on 74 plays. Suh chased McCoy on a third and 13 at the Nebraska 29-yard line and forced a throw out of bounds, and the game was over. Former coach Bo Pelini looked stunned as his team appeared to win its first conference championship since 1999.

Then the officiating crew determined that one more second should be added to the clock. Many argued that you could take every play in a football game and find a second here or there to add or take off the clock. The fact that this was the game's final play with national championship implications magnified the moment that much more. "I was a little bit numb to it all. I was [upstairs] in the [coaching] box," former special teams coordinator and defensive assistant John Papuchis said. "The emotion that was felt on the field and then the immediate aftermath of the locker room, I was not there for that because obviously the box is a lot more of a sterile environment anyway.

We're immediately trying to get the field goal block unit out on the field once they put the one second on the clock. What's crazy is when you go back and watch the replay of even the field goal, Suh almost blocked the kick."

And besides costing Nebraska a conference championship, the one second added back to the clock tarnished one of the best defensive performances ever. "For a long time, my memory and the way I thought about that game was more painful, and it was a negative thought," Papuchis said. "I've grown to appreciate what that performance was, especially for Suh, but really for all the guys. That was a really, really talented Texas team. I went back and I've watched it a couple times in the last couple of years, and that was a group of guys that we played as hard as we possibly could have played and was probably one or two plays away from winning the game. Just heartbreaking, disappointing that didn't happen that way because I think the whole legacy of what we were able to do at Nebraska and what Bo did at Nebraska would've been different if not for that close loss."

The loss to Texas also set the stage for the summer of 2010 and the friction that Nebraska felt with Texas, ultimately leading to the Huskers leaving the Big 12. What if Nebraska won the 2009 Big 12 championship? Would it have been as eager to leave the Big 12?

Regardless, Texas was looking around. The Longhorns either were going to leave for the Pac-10 then or create a TV network with ESPN that would give them a financial advantage no other Big 12 team would have. They landed their own TV network but ultimately didn't jump ship until joining the SEC, where they started play in 2024. Texas' craving for power and money, though, was the demise of the original Big 12, which added a unique rivalry piece to Nebraska's history.

20

Iowa

WHEN NEBRASKA JOINED THE BIG TEN IN 2011, ITS TRADITIONS and rivalry games were gone against Oklahoma, Colorado, and Texas. The Huskers needed a new ear-marked rivalry for obvious reasons, and Iowa made sense. Of the Big Ten teams, the Hawkeyes are in the only bordering state to Nebraska. The name Cornhuskers was actually taken from Iowa after Iowa switched to the Hawkeyes. Former *Lincoln Journal Star* sports editor Cy Sherman started referring to Nebraska as the Cornhuskers in 1900. Before that they were the Bugeaters (1892–99) and the Old Gold Knights (1890–91).

There was limited history from 1947 to 2011, as the teams played only six times. From 1891 to 1946, they met 35 times. "It was very difficult to get Big Ten teams to schedule Big 8 teams," former Nebraska play-by-play announcer and historian Jim Rose said. "Big Ten teams typically did not play Big 8 teams. It was very rare."

Iowa and Nebraska may have shared a border, and both were called the Cornhuskers at one point, but philosophically their views on football were much different. Big Ten schools held an academic level of prestige over the top of the Big 8. They did not believe in allowing partial academic qualifiers and junior college players into their schools. Teams like Nebraska and Oklahoma did, which gave them recruiting advantages in that era because of lesser admissions standards.

From 1979 to 1982, the Hawkeyes and the Huskers met each year, representing their first matchup since 1946. Hayden Fry had just gotten to Iowa, and Tom Osborne was in his seventh season as Nebraska's head coach. The series was scheduled because of former Huskers head coach and then athletic director Bob Devaney's relationship with Iowa athletic director Bump Elliott. They both grew up in Michigan and had many common connecting points. "Bob and Elliott were friends," Rose said. "Bob did a lot of that. His personal relationship with people got a lot of games scheduled. That also got a home-and-home with Alabama scheduled in the 1970s. It was just one of those things that he was able to do, and that's the way a lot of scheduling was done then. You scheduled a game, and then the networks would pick it up, whereas more like today the networks decide about non-conference games, and they're very involved."

Nebraska won three out of those four games, falling to the Hawkeyes only in 1981, the year Iowa played in the Rose Bowl. It was a 10–7 defensive struggle, as the Huskers' offense only put up 153 yards rushing and had just 13 first downs.

A few early seeds in the Iowa vs. Nebraska rivalry were planted over the four-game series. Osborne signed both running back Roger Craig and tight end Jamie Williams out of Davenport (Iowa) Central in 1978 and 1979. Meanwhile, Iowa signed one of its best all-time players from Nebraska during that era in 1982—linebacker Larry Station from Omaha (Nebraska) Central. "John Melton was a great recruiter, and Roger Craig and Jamie Williams were a package deal," Rose said. "There was a little tension. The other thing that Hayden Fry used to say quietly was, 'Well, all you have to do to be eligible in Nebraska is fog a mirror.' The Big Ten had some higher academic requirements, which is true, but that was a shot at Nebraska.

"It was a bigger deal if you were recruited by Nebraska in the 1980s. There was really no comparison at the time between the two programs until after Hayden got there. In the '70s if you had Iowa and Nebraska recruiting you, you didn't go to Iowa; you went to Nebraska. When Hayden got there, he was getting guys. He out-recruited us for Tavian Banks, who was a *Parade* All-American back from Bettendorf [Iowa]. Nebraska went hard for Tavian Banks, and he committed to Iowa and played very, very well for them. He was a really good back, but they had a different style of offense. They didn't run the option. They ran a pro-style. They were getting quarterbacks that were better. It was just a very, very different setup because we were in different leagues, and you'd rarely see them, but we did recruit their guys, and Hayden didn't like that. We would go over there and use our cache to get guys. Hayden didn't like that. He ordered Bill Snyder to go into Omaha and start looking for guys. He got a couple: Sean Ridley, Larry Station. Iowa got a couple, but there was always this bias against the Big 8 and the Big 12. It wasn't written down anywhere, but it was just understood that I'm better than you because I'm in the Big Ten, and yes, maybe you're really good at football, but we're a better university and a higher grade of people. That was the very idea there."

Fast forward to July 2011 in Chicago. Leadership from both schools got together that summer to promote the new series: the Heroes Game. There was even a corporate sponsor, as

Des Moines-based grocery store Hy-Vee was the initial present-ing sponsor of the game, which honored different unsung heroes from the two states. Top executives from Hy-Vee attended the press conference at the McCormick Place Convention Center in Chicago.

None of it felt natural. The start of the Heroes Game series in 2011—and the so-called rivalry—felt forced and very cor-porate. "It probably ruffles feathers me saying this. We didn't really see it that way or at least I didn't see it that way," former Nebraska defensive coordinator John Papuchis said. "They were a team that we played at the end of the year, and we beat them three out of four times. We felt like we were better than they were and we probably should have beat them all four times. In 2013 they came in and they were ready to roll. I don't know if at that time our players necessarily looked at it that way. In 2011 they came to Lincoln, and we beat them, I felt like, pretty handedly. [In] 2012 we had to win the game to win the Big Ten West, '13 they beat us, and then in '14, we beat them in a memorable road comeback, but I don't know that our kids at that time looked at it that way in terms of like a major rival."

It wasn't until after that 2014 game that things took off. The Huskers held a decisive 3–1 lead in the series. They had just beaten the Hawkeyes 37–34 in overtime. Former head coach Bo Pelini was fired after that game by athletic director Shawn Eichorst. "Our kids showed great character and resiliency in a tough environment," Eichorst said. "So it did play a factor. But in the final analysis, I had to evaluate where Iowa was. We weren't playing for a conference championship, and neither was Iowa. I have great respect for Iowa. It's a great institution and a wonderful football program. But in the final analysis, their record was where it was, and ours was where it was. Fair enough?"

It was that statement by Eichorst that actually jolted the rivalry. The Hawkeyes would go on to win the next seven games from 2015 to 2021. "The last thing you need to do is add any more fuel to their fire," former Nebraska and Iowa defensive line coach Rick Kaczenski said. "Being in both strength rooms, being in both staff rooms, being at both universities, that's going to come up every year that they play. That was a shot. I've said some dumb things over the years. The last thing that you need to give any successful program, any successful head coach, is any more fire. It was just something that didn't need to be said."

In 2017 Eichorst and former head coach Mike Riley even tried to get the league to take the game off Black Friday, citing that playing such an important game on one less day of rest and preparation was a disadvantage. "Since moving to a nine-game conference schedule," Eichorst said in September of 2017, "it makes sense from a student-athlete health, safety, and welfare perspective to play on Saturday at the end of the regular season."

NU has played every single Black Friday on national television since 1990. Before 1990 they played on either Black Friday or Thanksgiving Day nine times from 1965 to 1989. The Big Ten was going to move the Minnesota game to the final week of the year, but because of COVID schedule changes, the game with the Huskers and Hawkeyes remained on Black Friday in both 2020 and 2021. "When I was at Iowa and Nebraska and we talked about Black Friday, we thought Iowa and Nebraska, as we got into the conference, would be playing for something," Kaczenski said. "We thought about how special Black Friday could become with where both programs were and what that game could become. That was the ultimate goal: playing Iowa on Black Friday. We should be playing them to go to the conference championship."

Former Huskers quarterback and graduate assistant coach Joe Ganz is now tight ends coach at Middle Tennessee State. So he has some unique insight on the series and how things took a turn after Eichhorst's words in 2014. During a recruiting visit at a high school in 2021, Ganz ran into the Iowa offensive coordinator (at the time) Brian Ferentz, the son of head coach Kirk Ferentz. "We got talking, and he was asking about [the rivalry] and he's like, 'Let me tell you something. The best thing that the University of Iowa had happened to us that year was that Nebraska fired Bo Pelini,'" Ganz said. "'That was the best thing that happened to us because we couldn't move the ball an inch on you guys, and you guys were a really good team, and we knew we had a battle.'"

By 2025 Iowa and Nebraska will meet for the 15th year in a row on Black Friday. Their Black Friday series with Colorado ended at the 15-year mark in 2010. It's taken some time to get to this point, but the rivalry between Iowa and Nebraska has finally taken off. Even interim head coach Mickey Joseph's 24–17 win against the Hawkeyes in 2022 added to things as Nebraska's players celebrated with the Heroes Trophy in Kinnick Stadium. The win kept the Hawkeyes out of the Big Ten Championship Game.

The rivalry is very different to how it was before 2011. "There was no history," Ganz said. "As players they didn't really care because our roster wasn't built with a bunch of Iowa kids either. There wasn't a bunch at that point. There wasn't a bunch of Nebraska kids on the Iowa roster. It wasn't like you had that going for it. It felt forced. I feel like, I think, right now it's a little bit more of a rivalry. All rivalries just take time, and you got to have some success on both sides."

Acknowledgments

VERY FEW PEOPLE GET TO LIVE OUT THEIR DREAMS. I AM fortunate to be one of those people. I often joke I have the best job in Nebraska. When I wake up each morning, it never feels like work. I'd probably do what I'm doing for free if it was not my job. For the past 25 years, I've been blessed with a front-row seat and a backstage pass to Nebraska football. I've experienced winning at the highest level to some of the lowest points in modern-day program history.

I have only missed one game—home or road—since 2000. It came for a good reason, though, as I was interviewing in Nashville for the job I still have today. When I first interviewed for my full-time job in the fall of 2003, Shannon Terry, the founder of Rivals.com, 247Sports, and On3, told me I was walking into an unbelievable opportunity. He wanted to make me the first full-time digital writer in the Nebraska market and still allow me to be on TV and radio. Terry recognized how powerful the Nebraska fanbase was and he wanted to invest in this market.

I was given a growing platform to talk about Nebraska football, as I own HuskerOnline, the largest online community of Huskers fans.

Through all of that, I've collected and built an unbelievable relationship with the people around Nebraska football. I've also been able to connect with Big Red fans all over the world. I've had conversations about Huskers football just about everywhere. From the streets of Dublin, Ireland, to Honolulu, Chicago, Kansas City, Arizona, Colorado, and Washington, D.C., Huskers fans are everywhere, and their craving and passion for information about the program is unlike any other fanbase in college football.

When Triumph Books approached me with this opportunity, it was a no-brainer. Nebraska's fans are the program's most important asset. My job is to give them exclusive and unique content about the Huskers. This book allowed me to connect with many people I've met over the last 25 years and share their stories. I was lucky enough to sit down with Tom Osborne, Frank Solich, Mike Devaney, and many others as I put together this book. The book allowed me to reconnect with many and capture stories never shared with Huskers fans.

Thank you to everyone who supported me along the way, especially my wife, Lisa, and daughters, Kit and Carly. Also, thank you to everyone who took the time to talk to me and make this book possible.